Painting a Visible Translation:

An Artist's Journey From Italy to Morocco

By Deirdre West

Table of Contents

Dedicated to my sister Jennifer,

Keep writing

Preface

5/07

"Now I know how a chick with big boobs walking into a bar feels."

I stifled a laugh as I looked over at Adrian. His dress uniform was spotless and his insignias of rank gleamed against his chest, but it was the medals he had won in battle which drew the eyes of the officers already collected in the banquet hall. Their eyes began at chest level and narrowed in speculation before slowly drifting up to check identity. The women in low cut, formal gowns seemed to attract far less interest. Far from flaunting the medals on his chest however, he believed he had only been doing his job and I felt sure this was the first time any of the other officers in his class were made aware of them.

"Do you need me to protect you?" I asked.

"Actually, as the organizer of the captain's ball I need to make my rounds. Make sure everything is coming together. Are you going to be okay if I leave you here alone?" In a room full of people you don't know, was what he didn't say. When Adrian was not attending classes for the captains course, he rarely felt social and I was always secretly glad his idea of a good time was not spending hours at a bar with friends.

"I'll be fine, good luck."

Of all of the captains, Adrian had been selected to plan and design the captain's ball, though as he had pointed out a month before, "Yeah, it's a big honor until something goes wrong, then guess whose neck is on the chopping block."

Adrian exhaled and I could see the military officer in him taking over, his attention already focusing on what needed to be done, "Thanks babe, I will see you when everyone sits down to dinner."

Before I could blink he was gone and I stood alone in the entryway balancing on high heels and reminding myself I could relax. I had no rank on my chest, therefore I was invisible. The only thing that marked my difference was the tattoo that, in my backless formal gown, was on full display for the first time since I had received it. As something I had spent a year designing, it was a piece of my art which used the canvas of my spine to trace from neck to tailbone in undulating curves. I could still remember the day I got it in Mexico and it was as though the murmur of the crowd around me faded and I could hear the distant music played by the bands in Aguas Calientes during Dia de los Muertos. Remembering that day, the rest of my travels and my art, gave me the courage to lift my chin and proceed in among strangers.

I walked through the room of talking officers taking a picture with my mind, the way the light fell from high placed windows to dust the forms of those gathered. I tried to envision how I would paint it, were I comfortable in dusty frayed travel clothes and safe behind the barricade of my paint brushes. I had found a job repairing watches and framing pictures for a shop on the military base. In my free time, in a spare room of Adrian's apartment, amid a sea of boxes, Adrian had allowed me to make a little studio. I felt however, like I had put my plans on hold. Part of me was trying on a mask to see if it fit and as much as I loved Adrian, it was starting to feel a little snug, maybe chafe around the edges.

In the corner of one of the banquet rooms I saw three soldiers standing together. They were immediately different from the other officers, not only because they did not have dates at their sides, but because their uniforms were of a different cut and color and their features and skin had a foreign cast. They seemed to look at the surrounding crowd the way I did, watchful, curious, wary. There was a wallflower quality to them, as though unsure of their reception, or the correct way to interact. Part of the captain's course acted as an exchange program and was open to select foreign officers. It was considered a great honor to be allowed to attend the course, though in their respective countries all of them outranked the captains in the room. Most of them had left wives and families at home in their countries, whom they were parted from for the duration of the six month course.

As I approached I thought of how out of place I also felt, as though my artistic goals marked me as much a foreigner as their uniforms marked them. I introduced myself and discovered they were from Morocco, Egypt, and Turkey. Countries, I had always dreamed of visiting and I peppered them with questions, sharing the places I had visited and my future dreams of travel. As they described their homes, their eyes glowed with memories and their rigid postures began to relax.

When Adrian appeared at my elbow to check on me he was surprised to find me laughing and talking, as though to old friends. As he led me to our table I whispered, "Have you considered going to Morocco during your upcoming leave? We could see snake charmers in Marrakesh, ride camels into the Sahara! Then there are the pyramids of Egypt!" I sighed, "Imagine standing on the banks of the Bosphorus in Istanbul."

"I could probably get permission to go to Morocco, Egypt is a lot less likely. Al Qaida would love to capture an American officer on vacation. I have considered Morocco, though going to a Muslim country right before I get deployed to one..." He smirked at me and shook his head as though he was amused he was even considering it. I had hope however. Adrian, like me, rarely did the expected or easy. He rubbed his thumb gently against the bare skin of my lower back, "We will talk about it later. Thanks for making the foreign students feel included. I was having a hard time getting over to them."

"Trust me," I whispered, "I was having a great time." As I fixed a polite smile on my face and nodded at the others at our table, I couldn't help but feel like I was seen as an extension of Adrian. Who I was, was not as valued as whom I was with and my appearance, manners, and speech would all reflect on him.

Adrian was a career soldier and saw each officer as a competitor for coveted promotions. The pomp and politics of military life were not for him but military tactics and history were his passion. He had confessed to me once that deployment, in spite of the violence and fear, had begun to feel more comfortable to him than trying to live among civilians back home. I couldn't imagine him ever happy behind a desk. He craved action, to be useful, fighting shoulder to shoulder with his men, trying to make a difference. Whereas I, I felt more comfortable behind my canvas, trying to understand the world with my paintbrush. I had been traveling since I was a child but I fell in love with travel when I was twenty-one and journeyed to Florence, Italy to spend a year training at the Florence Academy of Art.

That night, after I kicked my high heels into a tangled heap in the corner and stretched my aching feet, I went through my journals trying to remember when it all began...

Florence, Italy: Beginnings

"'Imagine a pair of woman's lips,' Mogor whispered, 'puckering for a kiss. That is the city of Florence, narrow at the edges, swelling at the center, with the Arno flowing through between, parting the two lips, the upper and the lower. The city is an enchantress. When it kisses you, you are lost, whether you be commoner or king.'"
–Salman Rushdie, Enchantress of Florence

9/00

The sun is out and filters down through the trees and the shadows of pigeons chase themselves on the ground. I cannot bring myself to stay inside and so write from atop a low stone wall bordering a small piazza. Every line of the old buildings around me can be described as sculpture and to me it is age and history that makes them beautiful, the weathered cobblestones underfoot, the stained walls soaring above. Every morning I wake up and cannot believe I am in Florence.

The Florence Academy of Art set me up with an apartment on Via Dei Bardi, which was where the noble families had their palazzos before the Nazis blew them up during World War II. A man who used to be the Italian instructor at the school, now sublets his apartment to students. As the secretary had walked up the stairs to show it to me she had apologized, saying that while it was fully furnished it was a bit run down and I might not like it.

Prepared to be disappointed I followed her as she unlocked a small, wood door off the hallway and led me into a living room with a twenty foot high ceiling. Huge windows set halfway up the front wall looked out over the walled garden across the street and rising from the floor were waist high antique, metal heaters. An upright piano rested against one wall and old worn chairs, sofas, piles of magazines and boxes decorated the room.

The apartment was immense, not only in height but in length. It spanned the width of the block with the windows from the living room looking out over Via De Bardi, and at the other end of the apartment, down a long hallway which passed a formal dining room, a kitchen and two bathrooms, were three bedrooms which looked out over a road parallel to Via dei Bardi. This same nameless road ran the length of the River Arno and the view from the bedrooms would have cost a small fortune had the apartment been one of the luxury hotels dotting the river banks. As it was, the room cost only $350 a month, which included the cost of all utilities. Compared to the astronomically high rent I had been paying in California, I thought sure there had to be a mistake, or at least a catch.

The apartment is currently empty and as more students arrive in town they shall be given the opportunity to rent here as well but because I was first, I had my pick. I fell in love with the middle room overlooking the Arno River. It has French doors that swing open to a waist high, wrought iron railing that keeps you from pitching forward and crashing through an arching lattice of vines and flowers one story below. Mold sprouts on one corner of the ceiling and plaster falls in a steady rain, so everything on that side is powdered white. I think the room used to be an open deck but was walled in as an afterthought because the bedroom floor is made of worn red flagstones and the ceiling is only ten feet high. As the secretary had warned, the apartment is dusty, cracks run up the walls and in every corner is a pile of faded crumbling books or a forgotten cardboard box.

The wiring is odd and faulty, if you turn on the washing machine at the same time as the hot water heater, the electricity will go off. Then you have to call the maintenance man, who lives elsewhere and does not speak English, to come and unlock the downstairs door so the breaker can be flipped and electricity restored. For all three people who will live here, there is only a waist high refrigerator and a hot water heater suspended over the bathtub. It only heats enough water for one shower; anyone else has to wait another hour before the next shower can be taken. There is no shower curtain, only a nozzle hanging from an improvised hook over the clawed, porcelain, bathtub and it seems impossible to bathe without soaking everything in the room. With the hot water heater overhead, it seems an ideal recipe for electrocution.

Yet as I lay in bed at night, the view from my windows is the dome of the Duomo lit up against the night sky and the reflection of city lights shining up from the flowing water of the Arno River. In the morning when the sun rises, its first golden rays light up my room, and outside the swallows dip and glide. The climbing vines have escaped the trellis to tap on my window and the air blown off the Arno is new and fresh.

Only a day after I moved into the apartment I was sitting on a park bench reading my guide to Florence and enjoying the sounds of pigeons when a man sat down next to me. He told me he was originally from France but was teaching photography in Florence. He gave me a few pointers about places to eat and things to see. Then he asked if I'd like to go for coffee or hot chocolate in three hours after he got off work. I agreed because after struggling daily with my Italian, it was nice to speak to someone in English. I thought he could give me an insider's perspective on Florence and it seemed harmless enough. After all I am only twenty-one and he looked to be in his early sixties, easily old enough to be my father.

We agreed to meet later and when he left I went to the museum of the Duomo. My favorite piece of art was a pietá by Michelangelo, one of his last sculptures completed before he died. The marble he used was darker and more golden then the stone he used for the David and it depicted the figure of Christ dead and sagging between two other figures who struggle to hold him upright. I can never get over the flesh, the sense of bone, mass and musculature. It seemed impossible the statue was carved from stone. I felt if I reached across the barrier and pressed my hand to Christ's side my fingers would slide over the pliable surface of skin, cool and not unlike the silk of marble but animate, the surface of something that had a life and spirit of its own.

When I met up with the professor I couldn't help but feel nervous, wondering if it was a good idea to meet up with a complete stranger, but I told myself not to be such an uptight American. The spirit of traveling is to make new friends. We went to his favorite café where he knew the waiter. The café was empty but he sat in a chair which was pushed so close to mine we were pressed shoulder to shoulder. It was right then, I realized I had made a mistake. He began to try to convince me to go to his apartment around the corner for an authentic spaghetti dinner that evening. I was trapped because earlier, when making polite conversation, I had confessed how free my days were since school hadn't started. He said because I was single and he had recently broken up with his French girlfriend there could be no reason why I shouldn't have dinner with him, then we would both "be alone no more."

I was shocked. I could not understand how I had gotten myself into the situation. I did not want to hurt him by being rude but I did not want to encourage him either. I even tried to pay for my hot chocolate by racing after him and ripping out my change purse when he rose to speak to his friend, the waiter, who was shooting me smug insinuating smiles, only to discover he had already paid. Of course, when a female allows a male to buy her a beverage, it can mean only one thing.

It was so odd. I realized, at one point, he was trying desperately to entertain me. A sweat had broken out on his forehead and he was beginning to stutter as he realized I was attempting to nicely turn down dinner and he couldn't figure out why. Was the situation somehow my fault?

It was like that guy I met in Rome. I agreed to take a picture of him in front of a few monuments, he bought me a beer at an outdoor café to thank me and before I knew it I was whipping my head to the side to avoid an unexpected kiss. Was there some passionate undercurrent I missed? Thinking about it later, they both seemed so lonely. The French professor especially, was so upset.

After spending a few weeks traveling around Italy with mom, getting used to how to get around and communicate, she has returned home and I am alone in Florence. The apartment echoes to my footsteps but I feel the silence peopled with my thoughts and plans. I don't feel lonely. I feel very intensely alive being here. Everything holds a fascination.

A note from the landlord informed me the gas oven is working, not that I know how to turn it on. I refuse to light it, after dad lost his eyebrows trying to light the one in Mexico and I don't have anything to bake anyway. I have no idea what to eat. I survived in California on Top Ramen with frozen peas: fast, cheap, easy to prepare, student food. I have no idea what to replace it with here. Even if I could afford to eat out every meal, I don't want to sit in a restaurant by myself. Yet to find myself starving in a country renowned for its food seems ridiculous.

At a tiny neighborhood shop, I bought a can of peas and back at the apartment I found two can openers. The first was so orange with rust it wouldn't turn. I didn't even try to use that, just threw it away. The second was coated with black slime and hadn't been cleaned in years, it was foul but I was desperate and scrubbed it as clean as I could. Damn thing was so dull I ended up hacking at the can and prying open half of it with a spoon. During dinner I discovered canned peas taste like baby food and the butter in Italy is unsalted and did nothing to improve the peas except make them greasy. Note to self: do not buy canned goods or butter and must learn how to cook.

Hunger drove me to further explorations and I found an outdoor market the next day hidden in the neighborhoods selling fresh fruit and vegetables, shoes, dishes, linens for beds, and an adjoining warehouse which housed meat and cheese stalls. Pan sheets were filled with rows of rabbit hearts, pig heads hung from meat hooks and large baskets sat on the floor full of salted fish. I have no idea what to do with most of it. Perhaps the meat would seem less frightening wrapped in plastic and stamped with 'USDA approved' but it isn't. Plus, if the papers back home are to be believed, mad cow disease is beginning to sweep Europe. It is starting to seem like a good time to become vegetarian.

I sat on the steps of the Santa Maria del Carmine to rest. Inside, the Capella Brancacci is famous for Brancacci's frescoes which inspired Michelangelo to make drawings of them for study. It was on one of the very steps where I sat that Michelangelo's nose was broken by another sculptor for saying something arrogant.

The sense of time held in the city of Florence serves to make me feel very small and insignificant. Yet, looking at Brancacci's frescoes I could not help but feel a sense of connection through art which seems eternal next to the short span of human life. All artists speak through their art and Brancacci spoke to generations of artists. When I consider the power of his art to influence and shape the thoughts and lives of those who saw it, I cannot help but feel there is an inherent responsibility for artists to continuously seek knowledge, to perpetually strive to refine their craft and to consider the message their work is sending.

As I sat on the steps surrounded by the sound of people passing, I closed my eyes and lifted my face to the warmth of the sun. It would be easy to spend the last weeks before school starts, exploring Florence but I will have an entire year to uncover her secrets. The daring thing would be to test my travel knowledge and catch a train heading south, maybe get lost in the heart of what was the Roman Empire.

Chapter 1

Rabat: A Gateway to Adventure and Pirates

"What would you do then before you die?
I'd walk out the door to destinations unknown,
spending the sum of my breaths
in one extravagant gesture."
–Andrew X. Pham <u>*Catfish and Mandala*</u>

"No matter how many there may be in our family, no matter how many friends we may have, we are in a certain sense forced to lead a lonely life, because we have all the days of our existence to live with ourselves. How essential it is then, in youth to acquire some intellectual or artistic tastes in order to furnish the mind, to be able to live inside a mind with attractive and interesting pictures on the walls. Learning is an ornament in prosperity, a refuge in adversity and a provision in old age."
–Aristotle

9/07

The light winked off of the chandelier's hanging crystals and burned a constellation of miniature stars onto the dry tiled fountain below. In my mind I could still see the austere barren waiting rooms of the JFK airport. As I smoothed the cover of the passport clutched in my hand after a sleepless night on the plane, I felt lost and dazed.

When I reached the front of the line, the customs official frowned down at my paperwork. I had declared my profession as a waitress, merely one job picked from an eclectic résumé, and he did not know what that was. I found myself rethinking my life as I tried to explain the function of a waitress in as simple of English as I could. My father had always told me if I didn't finish college, I would spend the rest of my life working at either a gas station or waiting tables in a diner. Of all the places in the world, a sometimes waitress, and most of the time struggling artist, I had wound up in Morocco, one of the few nations in the world still ruled by a king.

I had originally become interested in Morocco while studying in Italy nine years earlier. A Moroccan dating a friend of mine from art school had told us vivid stories about the beauty of his country. At the time, to a twenty-one year old girl newly away from home, it had seemed an impossible, frightening trip to a Muslim nation perched at the very tip of northern Africa. It was a far cry from the refined museums and soaring cathedrals of Florence. Like most Americans, I had seen *Casablanca,* a film set in the coastal city of Morocco during World War II with the film noir romance of Humphrey Bogart defying the French and assisting the local rebels while exhaling moody, atmospheric clouds of cigarette smoke. The movie held little of Morocco, being filmed in entirety on a lot in Hollywood.

In later years I was inspired by the art of Jean Leon Gerome and his prayer scenes from atop rooftops with swarthy turbaned men bowing low to a dusky sky. As a child, I had an illustrated children's version of the story of Aladdin's lamp and around each brilliantly colored illustration were repeating geometric patterns, swirling like calligraphy. To combine with my romantic ideals were CNN headlines and the post 911 view of a western hating east filled with potential terrorists on every corner, just waiting for a lost American tourist. I was dismally aware of the fact I did not speak either of the national languages: French and Arabic.

Once in the taxi heading away from the airport I realized I had no idea what the currency conversion was from dollars to dirham and while the taxi rate to downtown Rabat had been posted in the airport, I had no idea what it converted to. Outside, palm trees were dwarfed by mosque towers and billboards whizzed by covered in Arabic script. I leaned over and rested my head against Adrian's shoulder and as he smiled down at me, I felt a warm rush of relief that I was not alone.

Adrian and I were dropped off outside of the walls of the medina, the old original city, and pointed across the street to the entrance. I stood and stared after our departing taxi in confusion until I remembered traffic was not allowed inside the medina walls, somewhere inside of which was the hotel I had booked. As I crossed the road burdened with luggage like an unrealistically packed donkey, oncoming traffic careening chaotically toward me, I felt the veil of unreality lift from my eyes. I was bombarded by exotic food smells, a chaos of noise, and stares from people passing by. We walked by a man sitting on the pavement selling plastic toys and a careening Osama Bin Laden gadget raced by with a motorized President Bush in hot pursuit.

I forced myself to focus, to look for the sign displaying my hotel's name, but I was constantly distracted by a fusillade of sensory images and smells. The buildings in the medina were whitewashed stone with accents of yellow and turquoise, into which were set imposing dark wood doors and shuttered windows. We passed the foot alley the hotel lay down and had to backtrack as I squinted at the tiny map from my guidebook.

Finally, a small stained sign advertised the name I had memorized and I stepped beneath it into a closet-sized room which strained to accommodate a battle scarred, wood desk. A thin, nervous man appeared and found our names in a worn notebook. Then, with barely a pause to catch my breath, I was climbing flight after flight of stairs behind him, deep into the gloomy bowels of the building.

A little later I collapsed on a lumpy but clean bed as exhaustion began to settle in. The walls around me were painted a deep, garish, fuchsia pink and the late afternoon light crept in through the slats of half-closed wooden shutters. Outside on the street a man sang in Arabic, a series of droning phrases repeated over and over, that dipped and soared on invisible sound currents like the elusive shadow of a gliding swallow.

I had already washed off the worst of the journey's sweat and dirt at the corner sink but felt minimally refreshed. There was supposed to be a shower on the roof but upon exploration I had found all of the doors at the top of the stairs were padlocked. The public toilet next door was nothing more than a hole set in a gleaming tiled floor with a bucket and water tap next to it for flushing. I found using it to be a precarious slippery business and was grateful to have packed a small supply of emergency toilet paper.

A moan issued from the spread-eagled form next to me, "God, it's hot. I can't believe, after over twenty hours on a plane, this is the hotel you reserved for us. I am definitely, picking out tomorrow night's hotel."

I sighed, "This hotel was in my budget. I did give you a copy of the itinerary and if you remember, I asked you to let me know if there were any changes you wanted to make. I did have to plan this whole trip on my own."

"And I'm grateful, but believe me babe, if you'd ever been deployed you would understand. You spend enough time living in really basic spartan living quarters. When you go on vacation all you want is a few luxuries. Like air-conditioning and a shower, those two things would be great right now." Adrian raised his head up briefly to look at me before dropping it back down with a defeated 'thunk.'

I gritted my teeth and reminded myself yet again, that traveling with someone else was going to take getting used to. Compromises would have to be made; my personal budget would have to be readjusted. I wasn't traveling by myself anymore, there was Adrian to consider.

Seven months before we had set off down the Alcan Highway on Valentine's Day, an adventure decorated with cigar wrappers, old coffee cups, three different road atlases and a flurry of blowing snow. That first day on a bathroom break, made in the middle of a blizzard, he had knocked on my window and with a grin pointed behind him to where he had peed my name in the snow next to a heart. It was a valentine that seemed to sum us up, unconventional, unpredictable, hilarious, and never boring. I didn't get out in Washington, Oregon, or in California, wasn't left on the side of the road in New Mexico, Nevada or Texas. I was amazed to find myself still squinting over maps in Louisiana. When we arrived at his assigned post, he had immersed himself in his studies and in his free time we had visited civil war sites and explored the south. Adrian had sponsored a visiting Major from Morocco and as they became friends he had encouraged us to visit his country. When seven months later, Adrian's captains course finished up, it was nearly time for him to deploy again. There was just enough time for us to take a vacation.

Neither of us had wanted to be stuck on a package tour, surrounded by fellow tourists and babysat by a guide so I had poured over a guidebook to Morocco and patched together an itinerary. I had originally thought staying in the medina would give us a more authentic Moroccan experience; unfortunately I had not taken into consideration my companion's more upscale expectations.

It was still early afternoon and in order to beat jet lag I calculated we would need to stay awake at least until evening. "Come on, if we don't get up now, we won't get up, then we will be twice as tired tomorrow," I said. Adrian sighed as he rose and twisted in place until his back gave an audible pop. Between the weight of his body armor in Iraq and the constant hits he had taken in his vehicle from IEDs, he suffered from constant neck and back pain. It was something he was afraid of getting looked at for fear it would keep him out of active duty and penalize his career.

As I rubbed the scar on my wrist from surgery, I reflected once again on how it was a choice I didn't understand. There were so many things we couldn't talk about. His views on the role of the military and the United States involvement in the Middle East were the exact opposite of my own. I didn't understand how he could enjoy a career that required him to follow orders without question and dictated nearly every aspect of his life both on duty and off. I felt that as a soldier he was a small cog in a vast machine that used its parts and discarded them when they were broken. The machine felt no loyalty towards the elements that kept it running, though those same elements were expected to give unquestioning loyalty and their very lives in return. Yet, the military was as much a part of him as painting was a part of me. I couldn't imagine him being happy doing anything else and I knew that to love him I had to accept every aspect of him, even those I could not understand.

Back outside, we made our way through the narrow streets of the medina. Clouds of steam and smoke rose from store front grills and racks of clothes rustled in a spice perfumed breeze. Underfoot an army of skinny cats with the occasional crying kitten wove through legs, scurried behind discarded boxes, and feasted on piles of scraps. Adrian put his sunglasses on in an automatic gesture because otherwise people stopped to stare and point at his vivid blue eyes. In contrast, as a woman escorted by a man, I found eyes skittered past me as though slipping across a pane of glass. I was studiously ignored.

We passed a variety of food stalls, most making fried meat and egg sandwiches. I felt sure my stomach must be audible to everyone in spite of the market's din and I grabbed Adrian's arm to make him stop. With an experienced eye he selected a large fried crepe hot from the grill that had cheese, onion, peppers, tomato, potato, and cornmeal in it. I gasped as it burned my fingers and ignored the grease which seeped through the wrapping to mark my skin as I ate.

We continued exploring until we emerged from the maze of the medina into an aggressive slap of sunshine. Before us, silhouetted against a white hot sky, was the formidable bulk of the Kasbah des Oudais. Its perch high on a bluff overlooking the body of water named the Oued Bou Regreg made it ideal as the former lair of a ring of bloodthirsty pirates who attacked boats coming into the Atlantic and Mediterranean. The corsair fleets, the "Sallee Rovers" specialized in the plunder of merchant ships returning to Europe from West Africa and the Spanish Americas and were practically impregnable in their fortified castle. They eventually established their own pirate state, the Republic of the Bou Regreg.

The open courtyards within the Kasbah were home to the Andalusian Gardens, laid out by the French during the colonial period. We were able to wander through them and peek into the entrance of the oldest mosque in Rabat.

Every time we paused to take pictures a Moroccan woman would come up to me offering to make henna designs on my hands. The ornate, burnt-umber henna designs were used primarily for special occasions like during a pre-wedding woman's party or at the beginning of the holy month of Ramadan. Hands decorated with henna represented the hand of Fatima, the Prophet Muhammad's daughter. At the time, I thought nothing of the women offering to paint my hands thinking it just another gimmick to separate tourists from their money. I did not realize until later I had unknowingly planned our trip right before the beginning of Ramadan.

Back at our hotel we endured a long night in which we realized it was too stuffy to keep our shutters closed, but too noisy to keep them open. The next morning, while walking to the train station, a sudden premonition had me stop at a bakery for food. It was an upscale place with a long glass case showcasing row upon row of pastries. I started to point at what I wanted but at a look from Adrian I dropped my left hand with a sigh and freeing my right indicated a flaky crusted pastry with an egg base and a topping of cheese, tuna, mayonnaise, black olives, barbecue sauce, and shrimp. It was a constant struggle for me to remember not to touch or point at anything with my left hand. It was considered extremely rude because in Morocco the left hand was reserved for use in the bathroom and therefore considered unclean. Traditionally thieves in the Middle East had their right hands removed as punishment which ensured ostracism from society.

At the train station we stood in a long line to buy tickets and as I watched, four Moroccan women ducked under the rope barrier, line jumping to the front. To my surprise an irate security officer appeared and yelling, chased them to the back of the line. I was impressed because in Mexico no distinction was made between the people in line first and the line jumper, the most aggressive person was always served first.

At my suggestion we bought two second class train tickets and I did not realize the enormity of my mistake until we found ourselves packed shoulder to shoulder in the passageway of a rail car with no air conditioning or ventilation for the next two and a half hours. Any time a person vacated a seat to get off the train an aggressive Moroccan woman would shove her way to the available seat first, often deploying her children to key points in the car to wait for openings. Standing in the narrow aisle with all of our bags we constantly had to press against the wall to allow people to squeeze past. With no way to get to a bathroom, I tried not to drink any water but stood soaked in sweat getting more and more dehydrated.

I finally pulled out some mint gum giving a piece to Adrian on one side of me and a young Moroccan man pressed on my other side. The Moroccan looked surprised at my silent offer but when I nodded, he took a piece with a small smile. The sweet mint taste pushed back my headache for a little bit and made the heat temporarily more bearable.

I had planned on us spending the night in Fes but an hour before it, as the train rumbled to a pause in Meknes, I caved in. A pulse pounded through my skull, each breath brought a stale sweet taste of overheated flesh which whispered over my cracked lips. I could barely summon the energy to shoulder my pack and turn to the scowling statue at my side. Adrian stared down at me, his shirt soaked to the waist, lips pressed in a tight line. “Come on, we’ll get off here,” I said.

Once in the relative cool of the station I looked down at my smudged itinerary in despair at the budget hotels I had listed and did not dare mention. Adrian took over. He strode up to the nearest loitering railway porter and interrogated him in an explosive volley of Arabic punctuated by an array of hand gestures. The porter answered by way of turning and pointing down the street. Without more than an impatient look over his shoulder to ensure I was following, Adrian stormed down the sidewalk pausing only once to adjust his direction in order to follow a group of well-heeled tourists. I panted in the heat, dragging my bags behind me and felt as though my every step was mired in thick black molasses. I sent up a small prayer of thanks for the foresight that had me eat earlier, without which I would surely have collapsed in a pathetic sniveling heap on the nearest street curb, unable to go farther.

With a determined air, Adrian examined the chrome finished, gleaming monolith of a modern hotel front that the tourists had disappeared into, and compared the invitation offered by its dark tinted windows to the recommended hotel further down the street. A glance back at me seemed to make up his mind and he vanished into the lobby. The room boasted air-conditioning, quiet, and I almost cried when I saw the attached western style bathroom complete with toilet paper, wrapped soap, and shower. For the rest of the afternoon we lounged in cool machine air processed bliss until finally venturing out for pizza at a ritzy overpriced tourist restaurant where I scowled at the menu in disgust. Yet, I had to admit to myself, I was too exhausted to try to find somewhere else.

A few buildings down we found an internet café and as I puzzled over the strangely arranged keyboard I wondered how to best describe my first impressions of a Muslim country to my friends and family back home. How to explain the way conversations around me blurred into a sonorous rise and flow of intangible rhythms, an indecipherable sing-song chant. How the long, curving, elegant symbols which traced mazes and designs on signboards were no more than elaborate drawings to me. Adrian seemed my only link back to the western world I had come from. Were it not for him the outer world would flow around me in an incomprehensible dance and I would be left alone in my head with my own thoughts, moved by the lovely mystery of my surroundings, but untouched.

* * *

The next morning I woke refreshed, the cool thrum of air-conditioning stirred the curtains at the window yet I could feel a small knot of nervousness within me disturbing my peace. So far my itinerary had not worked out, my first hotel pick had been a disaster and my frugal choice of train class had backfired as well. The next item on my neatly typed sheet was a day trip to Volubilis, the Roman Empire's most remote base and the largest and best preserved Roman ruins in Morocco. Roman rule of Volubilis had lasted a little over two centuries until 285 AD when the garrison withdrew. Before the area had been colonized by the Romans, it had been the western capital of the Berber kingdom. Adrian had majored in military history in college and the history surrounding the rise and fall of the Roman Empire held a bottomless well of fascination for him. I hoped taking him there would redeem me as a trip planner in his eyes.

As we walked out of the hotel I rejected my earlier cost saving plan of trying to find a local bus and instead we backtracked to the train station to negotiate with a taxi driver. Adrian could speak a little Arabic from his time in Iraq, though we had agreed were he to be questioned on his knowledge of the language we were to say he had studied it in school, not that he had been a soldier fighting in the Middle East. He had made an attempt at growing out the sides of his hair as well as sporting a hint of a beard in the hopes of hiding his military background but there was no disguising the posture and bearing of an officer. In spite of our nervousness however, his knowledge of Arabic and customs had gone unchallenged, while proving helpful time and again.

He was easily able to negotiate a roundtrip to Volubilis and after an hour of driving, our taxi pulled up and parked in a dirt lot next to a row of other taxis. The drivers lounged in the shade smoking, a silent, watchful bunch awaiting the return of their charges as the engines of their slumbering vehicles ticked and cooled.

We bought tickets at the gate and walked past a gauntlet of locals offering to give tours of the ruins. They called to us in a mix of languages in an attempt to determine our nationality but after hearing the prices, we decided to look around on our own. We set off down a dirt path that meandered around rocky hills before fraying into several smaller unmarked trails. We turned our feet in the direction of some irregularly piled columns silhouetted against the sky and began to come across signs posted in French and English offering information on low crumbling walls, weather beaten stone steps, and wind haunted alleys. Some buildings had intact doorways which beckoned to interiors scattered with free standing pillars that held up only a ceiling of limitless blue sky. Other structures still had detailed mosaic floors which, in spite of being 2,000 years old, retained their color. The floors depicted scenes that whispered stories, themes, legends, tales in a chiseling of rock, and gave meaning to the bare, bleached bones of the near forgotten foundations.

We started being followed around by a man selling hats which he bore in a tall stack atop his head, as though wearing the elaborate crown of some long vanished indigenous tribe, or the horn of an extinct beast. In a mixture of French, the occasional word in Spanish and a bare smattering of English he offered to give us a tour. We declined but he dogged our steps like a trickling seam of shadow and dropped tidbits of information whenever we dared to pause to consider our surroundings. At last all pretense was dropped and we had a guide whether we wanted one or not. At his gesture a half hidden channel became a vast drainage and sewage system which spread unseen tentacles beneath the entire city and supplied water to the bath houses. He demonstrated with a stick the time telling features of a stone sundial and took us to a building filled with old olive oil presses.

We explored a music school, a brothel, a sacrificial temple, the remains of numerous shops and houses, and at the end of the main road cutting through the center of Volubilis, a huge stone arch erected in honor of the Severian emperor Caracalla. The arch dominated and split the horizon while behind it the land dropped away into the distant curve of rolling hills.

What a painting it would have made: the white gleam of the stones with foot high words in Latin carved into the top, set against the surrounding purple and gold of the fields. In spite of the temptation, I reminded myself that I had decided to spend the first two weeks of the month long trip sightseeing with Adrian, one last hurrah before his deployment to Afghanistan. In the following weeks when I was traveling alone, I could dedicate myself to painting.

For the first time since our arrival to Morocco Adrian became enthusiastic. He leaned over stone walls trying to get the best possible photographs of mosaic floors, posed in front of looming pillars, and crouched down to inspect stone tablets. The history buff in him took over and I mentally congratulated myself on planning Volubilis as one of our early stops. While everything about our surroundings was new and exotic to me, being submerged in a Muslim culture again, surrounded by the lilting tones of Arabic and the constantly broadcast calls to prayer, had quieted Adrian. I had seen him visibly retreat within himself under a blanket of weariness.

Finally, hot and tired we paid our guide and took our taxi back to Meknes. On the way, the taxi driver drove us through the town of Moulay Idriss, one of the country's most important pilgrimage sites. Moulay Idriss el Akhbar was the great grandson of the prophet Muhammad and in Volubilis he was considered one of Morocco's most venerated saints and the creator of Morocco's first Arab dynasty. His tomb lay in the heart of town, which made the town a sacred place of pilgrimage. A tourist could visit the town briefly during the day but were forbidden to stay overnight or to visit the tomb. Accordingly we drove through the heart of town staring out of the windows and did not stop.

We were dropped off in the very center of Meknes, Moulay Ismail's imperial city, at Bab el Mansour, an impressive monumental gateway set between the medina and royal palace. Originally the marble columns of Bab el Mansour had belonged to one of the buildings in Volubilis but had later been pillaged for use in Meknes. Above the gate was an ornamental inscription lauding the victory of Ismail and his son Abdallah, and that there was no gate in Damascus or Alexandria it's equal.

Inside was a reception hall for ambassadors beneath which were subterranean vaults thought to be a prison for Christian slaves. There were several thousand Christian prisoners used as slave labor at the time and legend had it if any died while at work they were entombed in the walls they were constructing. I found myself rubbing the scar on my wrist as I looked up at those towering stone walls and thought about how different things were for me. When I had become injured on the job, the cruise ship company had to compensate me for my time and medical bills. Those walls symbolized not only a different time but a completely opposing world to the one I knew. There was something worse than poverty; there was slavery, when someone else owned not only your body but the sum of the days of your life.

In the city of Meknes there were twenty gates, over fifty palaces and fifteen miles of exterior walls. We began to walk around using a tiny map from my book but quickly became confused by the lack of street signs and the number of narrow twisting alleys. We finally gave in and hired a horse drawn carriage with a French speaking guide. He managed the occasional word in English and Adrian was able piece together his Arabic in order to glean a sporadic kernel of information. The main benefit of the carriage ride, I swiftly realized, was not informative, it was the ragged canvas top that shielded our heads as we rattled down a network of walled palace corridors that were bathed in the smoldering eye of the sun.

On the tour we passed the grand Mausoleum of Moulay Ismail, the sultan who made Meknes his capital in the 17th century. He ruled from 1672-1727, and was known as one of the most tyrannical sultans in Morocco's history. This period was considered Morocco's last golden age and his reign saw the creation of Morocco's strongest army with a garrison force of one in twenty of the male population. His rule began in Fes with the display of 700 heads, most of them captured chiefs. Over the next five decades it was estimated that he was responsible for 30,000 deaths. He used to carry a weighted lance with him while inspecting progress on his buildings which he would use to bash in skulls, in order to encourage others. He was known to say, "My subjects are like rats in a basket, if I do not keep shaking the basket they will gnaw their way through. "

The route our carriage took us on, through the walled corridors by the palace, was a favorite ride of the Sultan who was pulled in a chariot drawn by his women or eunuchs instead of horses. Each of Ismail's palaces had underground plumbing well before Europe developed it. Unfortunately much of what we saw was the high outer walls of the palaces with only occasional lush glimpses of gardens or fountains through huge ornamented doorways and gates. The palace was closed to the public and I could only imagine what it must be like inside.

Afterwards we walked through an open air market, a dizzying display of foreign items, so exotic that I could not identify half of them. We bought some sweet bread from a cart literally crawling with bees and I ate a fresh date plucked from a golden stack by the swarthy keeper and offered to me as a sample. As the sweet sticky flesh of the date dissolved against my tongue I felt as though it carried the savor of time, a vision of marble pillars made whole against a blazing pure sky. Perhaps in another market in a time long past, another man reached down to offer a date with a flash of a smile, as though to share a singular treasure, a dizzying taste of Morocco.

In the Heart of the Roman Empire

My Dear Family, *9/00-10/00*

I write to you from a peaceful train which is slowly inching its way back to Florence. I managed to find a nonsmoking car and I share it with very few other travelers. I decided to use the remaining weeks before school to see more of Italy and went south. Traveling around Italy is still such an uncertain experience. Initially I always feel suspicious when I get on a train and sit down, like any minute, the sign next to the train will change and instead of going to Florence the train will decide to go somewhere else completely.

Before I left Florence, I was experimenting with buses and realized you never know how big a city is until you are on a bus stuck going in the opposite direction of where you wanted to go and you have no idea where you are because suddenly nothing is familiar. It is almost as though you stepped on a disguised space shuttle and emerged onto another planet. At such a moment you are painfully aware that all you brought with you is a bus ticket which is rapidly coming closer to expiration because believing yourself on a simple jaunt to the train station to investigate train schedules then back to the apartment, you failed to bring money or map. It would have been ten times faster if I had just walked.

I got to Rome without incident but have decided the city is far too big and intense for me. I was propositioned in both Italian and Spanish in one day; I understood the one in Spanish but didn't let him know that. I finally got a chance to sit down and this guy came up trying to speak to me in Italian and sell necklaces. I said, 'no grazie,' five or six times before he finally gave up and went away. I also can't count how many times people have waited until I was in the crosswalk, then slammed on the gas and tried to run me over. I am glad I came back to Rome to see things I missed the first time but was relieved to be heading on to Pompeii.

I returned to the Vatican and St Peter's Cathedral had less people in it then when mom and I went so I was able to look around more. I saw Michelangelo's Pieta, it seems much smaller in life. It was so beautiful in pictures that in my mind I expected it to be at least as tall as the David, but it was still gorgeous and I wish I could have touched it. It's funny how when you see something truly moving, you want to be a part of it, or to somehow stake a small claim on it. Something as simple as touching is proof that it is real and I can imagine other hands through time smoothing down the surface of those rich marble folds of cloth that adorn the Madonna, or caressing the delicate fingers of the hand of Christ.

There is something captured in the faces of that sculpture, which expresses so many things about humanity. In the sorrow and acceptance in the simple lines of Mary's face, Michelangelo caught the grief of a young mother losing her grown son, but the acceptance of a woman of faith for divine will. Christ's face has such a conflicting mixture of peace, serenity and the aftermath of suffering but it goes beyond the relaxed mouth and closed eyes. His very body speaks with the delicate sweep of muscle and gesture of his limbs. He is a grown man and yet Mary manages to hold the entirety of him on her lap, bearing his pain as well as her own. The curve of her form is fragile and yet there is such a resolute strength of spirit in her body and face. To me it goes beyond religion and speaks about people everywhere, going through life with their simple hopes and dreams. To think that such a beautiful thing was created out of a block of blank stone. Seeing things like this, every doubt in my heart is washed away and I realize art is an endeavor worthy of dedicating my life to.

I walked to the Coliseum and got to go inside at last. It seems so innocuous with its crumbling stone and the arena floor laid open in order to show off the construction of the lower levels. It is difficult to imagine it as a place of such brutal slaughter. The spectacle it must have been when it was still running, the snarls of lions, the scream of men and the roar of the crowd. It seems far smaller than I had imagined it to be but perhaps it only seems small compared to our baseball and football stadiums of today. Yet, some things don't change; people still like to be entertained.

The next day I traveled to Pompeii and it was as fascinating as I had thought it would be. I followed a tour group into a still intact building that used to be a bordello, there were erotic frescos on the walls of different sexual positions and in one dark closet sized room that I stumbled into I was nearly stabbed by the enormous erection of a life-size stone statue.

As I walked through the main gate of the city I tried to imagine all those people running down it and trying to escape as ash filled the air. Do you remember the time in Alaska when Mt Augustine blew and we woke up in the morning to see ash falling like snow? Time is very strange, it was unbelievable to touch the walls of buildings which are still standing and realize they are about 2,000 years old.

From Pompeii I took the commuter train to Sorrento, and then hopped on the first bus to Amalfi. The bus was so packed I had to stand for an hour while it careened around corners on the switchback roads. The bus drivers and roads are imported straight from Mexico. I was white, shaking, and turning green after my first Amalfi Coast experience. Imagine a road set on the edge of a cliff that drops straight down to the sea, and then imagine it so narrow it is barely big enough for two cars. The bus was so big that to go around the sharp blind corners it had to take up both lanes and sometimes back up to maneuver them. Every curve the driver came to he had to lay on the horn and hope no one came racing around the corner while the bus was taking up both lanes. Nuts, it was completely nuts, yet there were no dents or scratches on the buses. Maybe it is because the ones that make mistakes end up at the bottom of the cliff washed out to sea.

When I got to Amalfi, it was pitch dark and I had to hike to the next town of Atrani where my youth hostel was. I was too scared to make the walk on those roads in the dark so I chickened out and caught a taxi, even though it blew my budget. Once there, I immediately made friends with a girl in my room, Sophie from London, and two guys she had met, Shane and Mike from Alabama, and another American named Pete.

The next day we all went to the island of Capris together and spent the day walking around, peeking at stores, and admiring the villas that overlooked the ocean. What we really wanted to do was visit the Blue Grotto, one of the water caves which Capris is famous for. Even though the sun was shining and the sea seemed calm, the boat men at the dock told us the water was too rough and they couldn't take us. The water caves are right at the water line and to get in you have to lay flat on the bottom of the boat during low tide and ease in the opening.

On Capris the last boat to the mainland left at 5:20 pm, and if you miss it you are stuck on the island till morning. At 5:15 we walked to where we were dropped off at the docks that morning only to be told by a guy standing on the pier that our boat left from the other side of the marina. Swearing, I started to run, the others gamely trotted behind me but couldn't keep up, relying on me to get there first and keep the boat from leaving. Halfway there I was gasping for breath and getting dizzy because it was really far, and I panted to the guy closest behind me that I couldn't do it, I was going to be sick, so he wheezed past me. We caught the boat barely but even as the boat began to pull away from the pier we saw another tourist couple yelling and running, having made the same mistake we had.

That night one of the Canadian girls in my room sleep walked and woke in the morning in only her underwear on top of a pile of garbage in the street. We were all very glad that nothing bad had happened to her, and made sure to watch her closely at night after that. The next day my little group decided to stay at the beach but I wanted to go see the ruins at Paestum, which despite the long scary bus ride along the cliffs was worth it. They are the largest Greek temple ruins in Italy.

We met up that evening at a takeout pizzeria by the beach. I took a chance and ordered the Napoli pizza since this is the region where it is most famous and when I opened my box I was disappointed. At first glance there seemed to be no topping, not even cheese, only red sauce, but with one bite I realized I had made the perfect choice. It was delicately and deliciously flavored with spices and garlic, putting to shame every American pizza I have ever had that was loaded with cheeses, vegetables and meats.

Later we sat on stone steps drinking red wine out of paper cups and watching the rhythmic pull of the waves. It was Shabbat for the two Jews in our group and they performed a short ritual, singing Hebrew over their pizza and we all clicked plastic cups at the end of it. In our little group we had two Jews, one Agnostic, an Atheist, a nondenominational Christian and a Buddhist. We talked for hours about religion versus spirituality trying to discover shared beliefs.

We were all such separate travelers looking to find our way, experience new cultures and meet new people. I wish sometimes I could hold on to moments of shared connection like that with something stronger than memory. It was more than the darkness of the night, the lapping of the waves, the lingering scent of pizza, the murmur of voices; it was a feeling of momentarily understanding something much bigger than ourselves. When I think back on that night, it stands out with clarity over all of my other experiences. Even after I left the Amalfi Coast and we went our separate ways I tried to remember, to fix it all inside. Now it is fading, exactly what was said, even people's names, where they were from but I remember what we agreed upon in the end, close to midnight. Each of us is a shining light in the darkness. We should be beacons of hope to each other.

From the coast I caught the train north to Assisi and by the time I got there I was grouchy and starving, plus I couldn't find my change purse which I became convinced I had left at home. All I had was a 50,000 lira note and I needed to buy a bus ticket but the tabacheria didn't have enough change. I finally got some change from the train ticket booth and was outside, irritated; trying to stuff my money and ticket in my money belt. This guy in his seventies was staring at me, bending his head to watch me put my money away. So I said, "Scusa, is there a problem? What?"

He leered at me and asked if I'd like to have a coffee with him (in Italian). I am thinking, 'oh god, not this again,' so I said, "No grazie." I said it somewhat rudely hoping he would go away but he moved still closer and kept talking to me and leering, so I put my hand up in his face and walked away to a larger group of people standing by the bus stop. He left me alone finally. Then this other guy came and stood next to me. He was somewhat younger, probably early forties but by this

time I was really mad and I turned my head as if I didn't know he was talking to me and completely ignored him. Sophie, the girl from London, calls this 'blanking' as in, 'I couldn't believe what he was saying so I completely blanked him.' Anyway he finally got the point because he got in his car and drove away.

I was thinking, 'what?' I was wearing shapeless pants and a sleeveless baggy black turtleneck. They were hardly the sort of clothes to inspire passion. What is the deal with these men? All of them were easily old enough to be my father.

I finally caught the bus into town, had two slices of pizza and started to feel human again. My guidebook gave almost a street by street tour of Assisi, it was enormously helpful, otherwise I would have been so overwhelmed by the beauty of this town I would have wandered aimlessly for hours and got quite lost.

I stopped in a little shop where a man with white hair was selling watercolor paintings of the town and little lithographs on cards. I was admiring them out loud and considering buying a card to send all of you when it turned out he was the artist. I told him I was from Alaska, by way of apologizing for my poor Italian, and headed for the door to look at his postcards when he said beaming at me, "No, please, I wish to make a gift," and waved a hand at his lithographs. I protested but he insisted so I selected one and he kissed me on the cheek. The effect I seem to be having on older men is just... beyond explanation.

In the middle of town is the Temple of Minerva which has been converted into a church but inside it still has drains by the altar which were used for blood sacrifices in the old days. I also saw the Basilica of St Francis, which the town was famous for, set on what used to be known as the 'the hill of hell' because it was where criminals used to be executed. The cathedral is wallpapered with frescoes, all three stories of it, including the tomb of St Francis. In 1997 an earthquake brought down part of the vault and a fresco by Cimabue and killed four people. Can you imagine anything more crazy or horrible? It gave me the shivers being inside looking up at those beautiful paintings and imagining being squashed by one of them.

On the platform waiting for the train to Orvieto the next day, I met a 63 year old lady named Elaine from Ohio, also traveling alone, I helped her with her luggage when the train came because it doesn't stop for more than a few minutes, then we decided to pair up because we were going the same way. We got to Orvieto and the cheap place I was going to stay at was in pieces with a big restoration sign on it. Next choice was the nunnery but they weren't taking people either. By then I was frantic, I finally found a place with a single room with a bathroom, very nice and clean although more than I had planned to pay. Of course I got the one room with nothing but cold water; they are trying to fix it as I write so I can take a much needed shower.

* * *

I went on a one hour tour with Elaine of a few of the caves dug by the Etruscans out of the 1,000 odd caves under Orvieto. The town is built on an old lava flow, portions of which are a soft compacted ash that the people mined for and used as cement between the blocks of their houses. The caves were also used to house olive oil presses, stables, pigeon coops, temples, and during WW II, bomb shelters. The Etruscans subsisted mainly on pigeons in time of siege. Only once was there a successful siege of the town. Around 200 B.C. the Romans laid siege for two years and the people of the town must have finally run out of pigeons because they surrendered.

After the tour we had dinner in a restaurant in an underground cavern. Candles flickered from the tables and cast shadows on the rock walls. I had ravioli stuffed with cheese and black truffles. I can think of no words to adequately describe the taste only images: afternoon light on the confectionary pink and white marble of the church, a shadowed alley with a splash of flower blossoms cascading from windows onto cobblestones, the movement of wind in hanging vines down to stir tendrils of dark earth.

The next day Elaine went to Rome while I caught the bus to Civita di Bagnoreggio. I met a nice lady, Joan, who was as confused as I had been an hour earlier trying to find out information. The bus was leaving in five minutes, she didn't have a ticket, the bus driver wouldn't let her buy one from him, and the nearest tabacchi to buy a ticket at was four blocks away. The bus driver said he wouldn't wait for her to buy a ticket and there wasn't another bus for four hours. Observing this from my seat on the bus, I leaned forward and said, "You can have the ticket I bought for the trip back because I can buy another one when we get to Civita." She gave the bus driver a pointed look and sat across from me.

The bus let us off at the more modern town of Bagnoreggio and we walked through it to the other side where we crossed a long foot bridge spanning a gorge to the tiny isolated hill town of Civita. Inaccessible to cars, it has only fifteen full time residents, although a school of architecture sends students there to live and study the old Etruscan dwellings.

As we were walking through the tiny streets together, a little old lady came out of a garden and pulled us into her house. She didn't speak English but pointed out in my guidebook where she was mentioned and gave us a tour of the Etruscan grotto under her house that still had an old olive oil press. Her granddaughter was upstairs making bruschetta, using fresh homemade French bread toasted in slices, drizzled with olive oil, and garnished with tomatoes and garlic from their garden. The granddaughter poured a glass of wine and kicking back a chair sat down to talk to us. She spoke excellent English and told us about the area and the restoration being done on some of the houses. Her dad came in with some grape juice that was about to go through the fermentation process to become their latest batch of wine. She insisted we have a taste and it was different from anything I have ever had, very sweet but with a tangy bite, almost like the carbonation in soda.

The next day I hopped on the train back to Florence. I have roommates now, the smaller room has a Swedish girl in the sculpture program, and the other has a girl from Australia, in the second year painting program. Tomorrow is the first day of school. I miss you guys, I will write more later.

Chapter 2

Fez: The Perilous Lure of the Bazaar

"Fez is like a drug. It enmeshes you.
The life of the senses, of poetry,
of illusion and dream.
It made me passionate,
just to sit there on pillows,
with music, the birds, the fountains,
the infinite beauty of the mosaic designs,
the tea kettle singing,
the many copper trays shining.
The twelve bottles of rose perfume and
sandalwood smoking in the brazier,
and the cuckoo clocks chiming in disunion
as they please.
The layers of the city Fez are like
the layers and secrecies of the inner life.
One needs a guide." –Anais Nin

9/4/07

I watched as Adrian crossed the station lobby and stood in line to buy us first class train tickets to Fez. A small, round, shrouded woman attempted to push in front of him and he stared down at her, his posture suddenly formidable. I could not hear what he said but she tilted her head up, stepping back and I knew she was surprised by his knowledge of Arabic.

Instead of costing one dollar the tickets cost us two and in exchange we got assigned seats in an uncrowded air-conditioned car. Adrian struck up a conversation with a Moroccan man sitting next to us who told us where a better and cheaper hotel was than the one we had planned. He also recommended an English speaking tour guide who used to be a teacher and would meet us at our hotel, show us his tour license, and take us around the city in his car.

As I watched Adrian question the man, I realized Adrian's presence was a relief. Wherever we went people looked to him, spoke to him, solicited him and for once I was as invisible as I had always wished to be. His size and strength seemed a deterrent to most, next to him the Moroccan men seemed slight and small. At the same time, traveling with someone was like learning how to dance with a partner, the gentle rhythm of back and forth, the aggressive steps forward only to give way and sway back a few steps. I was no good at the giving way, relaxing my body into the spins and turns, allowing the arms of my partner to support the full weight of my body as he led me into a dip. I was too used to making decisions, taking charge and I struggled with myself to let go. To remember it was Adrian's trip as much as mine, a last taste of peace for him and we were supposed to be partners not opponents, dancing together, not separate.

Adrian and I exchanged a look as the man flipped open his phone and called his friend, the guide, to make arrangements. It was difficult to know who to trust. My guidebook had repeatedly warned against trusting seemingly friendly locals but I couldn't help reasoning to myself that a local would be far more knowledgeable then a guidebook. If he were to get a commission from setting us up with a hotel and a guide, what did it matter to us if we were satisfied with both? We needed help. Adrian despised every hotel my book suggested and we would need a guide for the labyrinthine streets of Fez's walled old town.

When we arrived in Fez he led us to the hotel and with each step I questioned my decision to trust a stranger. Yet when we walked into our hotel room I heard Adrian let out a sigh of relief behind me. The room was small but it was cool and clean, the AC a soft whir overhead, and a large TV sat in the corner. Having a TV on at night had taken a lot of getting used to for me. I was in the habit of curling up with a book before bed, but Adrian couldn't sleep without the TV on. He told me once that silence made him nervous; he started to listen for out of place noises instead of sleeping. In Iraq he had become used to the near constant backdrop of sound that came with an army at war.

"Happy?" I asked as I laid down my bag and eyed the TV with resignation.

He smirked, "Don't even pretend you are not excited by the Western style bathroom." I rolled my eyes but could not keep a smile from my lips.

Downstairs in the lobby we waited for our guide. I stood in front of a rack of postcards, slowly inspecting each one until I noticed a thin balding man who hovered nervously outside the hotel door. Tilting my head to one side I walked out and smiled in greeting, unsure if he was our man, and when he spoke it was in fluent English. I was disarmed by the pleasantries, his small jokes, his unthreatening demeanor and without realizing it I found myself in the midst of negotiations over price. Before I could blink the price was settled. It was a substantial amount more than we had planned to spend, but for an English speaking guide, a car, and a tour that promised to last nine hours, taking us even into the surrounding countryside, it seemed money well spent.

I darted across the street to buy a bottle of water then we were climbing into the back of his car. After a bewildering maze of streets strewn with a chaos of glinting, honking cars, the suburbs, then finally the countryside began to unravel around us. "First we begin with tour of factory of the pottery. You have not seen this yet in Morocco? No? Ah, it is very interesting. The owner will give you the tour, he speaks very good English. After, we return to old part of Fez."

We pulled into a walled courtyard and parked under an overhang, our guide got out and walked in a long ground eating stride to a group of men who lounged against the wall, eyeing us as we got out of the car. We were waved over as our guide spoke in a flurry to a man who separated himself from the others and approached us with a gesture of welcome. Outside in long rows, squares of grey clay baked in the sun and inside the first building we came to, two men sat up on platforms, each in front of a large pottery wheel deftly making pot after pot of clay.

I held up my camera in question to our new guide and he smiled, "Yes, take pictures, pictures are for free, but if you want them to smile, you have to ask." He turned and rattled off a stream of Arabic to a younger man who perched on a stool atop the nearest platform, the wet clay trailing through his fingers as it spun. He raised his head from his work with a questioning look, then his dark eyes drifted to me and a slow languorous smile spread over his lips.

As the wet clay slid through his fingers creating concentric rings and grooves, I wondered what he was thinking about. To a craftsman, was the motivation behind the work simply to provide the means for a living, or was there additional satisfaction in the unity and precision of the forms his hands created? Next to him was a very tall set of metal shelves packed with finished pots awaiting firing, each looked identical to the one next to it. Watching him work my fingers craved my brushes and paints.

The next room we ducked into was dominated by two huge kilns, big enough to stand up inside of and consisting of two levels. He explained the firing process as he led us through an adjacent door into a small enclosed space with no windows. By fluorescent light men carefully hand-painted perfectly proportioned geometric designs on pots and plates. He showed us how the colors of the paint changed dramatically after the design was finished and fired. Watching those men hunched over in that dim false light, I could feel the ache that must develop over time in the neck and eyes. Yet with the lack of jobs, it had to be considered good, steady work. Similar to Mexico, Morocco didn't have enough jobs to support its people so they traveled abroad for work, and then sent money home. More than 1.5 million Moroccans worked in Europe alone.

Outside under a roof, sat a row of men who were taking finished painted tiles and chiseling shapes out of them to be used in mosaics. The mosaics decorated the tops of tables and chairs and edged the frames of large mirrors that would be shipped out of the country. Even as we watched them, and their easy, efficient movements, they stole small glances at us. Hearing me ask the factory guide a question, one worker asked in Arabic if I was Moroccan. When Adrian replied I wasn't, the man shook his head and said I had the face of a Berber woman. The factory guide overheard and laughed, "Yes, if she was a Berber woman she would be worth at least 2,000 camels." Adrian's mouth twitched as he looked at me with skepticism.

"Yeah, 2,000 camels buddy, when are you going to pay up?" I asked. Adrian rolled his eyes as we were ushered into the factory store which had shelves of colorful vases, plates, bowls, salt and pepper shakers and cups. Even ceramic arms curled from the wall, sporting the henna painted hand of Fatima, fingers spaced to allow jewelry to be hung from them. It seemed far too early in the trip to be buying things, especially something breakable but the factory guide had taken his time to explain everything to us. We looked at each other and sighed. I wondered if this foreshadowed the rest of our day. Were we going to be expected to continuously purchase things in compensation of individual tours?

I realized the amount we had paid for our tour was perhaps not the final price, at the end of the day we would see how much had been really spent. We picked out a few small things then our original guide appeared to walk us back to the car. Driving back to the city we stopped to see the Merenid tombs on a hill overlooking the Medina of Fes. We took a few pictures then drove back into the center of town and parked outside of the medina.

A Medieval European traveler once described Fes as "a citadel of fanaticism" yet at the time it was the most advanced center in the world of medicine, mathematics, and philosophy. The city was founded by Moulay Idriss I, but it was his son Moulay Idriss II who really began the city's development by making it his capital and welcoming in refugees from Tunisia and Andalusian Cordoba. Those refugees established separate walled towns on both river banks and had provided superior craftsmanship for Fes's industrial growth. When Fes was conquered by the Merenids in 1248 they built a huge royal city Fes el Djedid, developing the Kairaouine University by building a series of medersas (colleges). They also decorated the Kairaouine Mosque and added a network of fondouks (inns). In the mid-16th century when the dynasty fell, the new rulers, the Saadians, preferred Marrakesh and Moulay Ismail despised the inhabitants of Fes so much he taxed them into poverty.

Fes was divided into three districts: Fes el Bali which was the core of the medina, and considered the largest living medieval

Islamic city in the world, Fes el Djedid which contained the Mellah, and the Royal Palace, and the third district, the Ville Nouvelle where our hotel was, the most modern area of town which began as an administrative area constructed by the French. We began our tour in Fes el Djedid in front of the main entrance to the Royal Palace, which was closed to the demanding tourists. The doors to the palace were hammered bronze with repeating raised designs, hand worked, yet in spite of their enormous proportions the patterns were perfectly symmetrical.

As we walked into the adjoining old Jewish quarter, the Mellah, we found ourselves on a glittering street lined with jewelry shops. Looping roped necklace chains winked in display windows, rows of glittering rings and bracelets were scattered over dark cloth. The honking vehicles were left behind us as we were absorbed into an equally chaotic rush of human traffic, peppered with animals and carts.

Mellah translated to salt in Arabic; thought to refer to the job given the Fassi Jews of salting the heads of the criminals before they were hung on the gates. Many trades were originally forbidden to Jews so they had little to choose from except money lending, which was against the law of Islam, or working as laborers. In 1912 when the protectorate was declared they came under the protection of the sultan who declared them to be just as Moroccan as Muslims. The Mellah, of Fes used to have a population of nearly 17,000 Jews but almost the entire population immigrated to the new Jewish state of Israel after Morocco became independent because the Jews felt they would not do as well under an Islamic government. Now only a few families remained in the Mellah, although a small community still lived in the Ville Nouvelle.

Religious tolerance was one of the laws of Islam, although religion and government were not considered separate structures in Morocco. Islam stated that people should be allowed to follow their own religion as long as they recognized the Muslim authorities who ruled the nonreligious aspects of life.

We crossed over into the old Berber quarter and walked into a warren of intersecting footpaths spiraling off from each other in a web-like pattern meandering through a covered bazaar crammed with shops, restaurants, workshops, mosques, dye pits, and tanneries. We were led through a maze of alleys narrow enough that we could continue only single file. The five story residences looming above us made the way dark and gloomy. Adrian became more and more nervous as the alleys became more isolated and feeling the tension curling off of him I understood for the first time how much we had to trust our guide not to take us somewhere deserted where we could be robbed.

Suddenly our guide waved us through an unlabeled door off a private walkway that we would never have found or ventured into on our own. I felt Adrian hesitate next to me and in that moment I knew we had to decide, did we trust our guide or not? Adrian clenched his jaw and gave me a small nod as he pushed past and stooped through the low entryway first. I followed and as I straightened up from the small cramped doorway I felt as though we had stepped into another world. We were in a large shop crammed floor to ceiling with intricately ornamented hand-worked brass and silver. The floor was decorated with a detailed tiled mosaic and above a huge ornate brass fixture hung from the elaborately carved wood and plaster ceiling.

As I explored the seven separate rooms, one devoted almost entirely to antiques, another to handmade knives and yet another to gleaming silver tea sets, I remembered the story of Aladdin. Only in Fes could there be a possibility of finding a wish granting brass lamp lying discarded in a heap of antiques. Which brought to mind the question, if all of your wishes could come true, what could the world hold of value? Aladdin had discovered that only when you lost everything were you able to truly appreciate what you had. Was the secret to wisdom and truth then, in loss?

Surrounding us were shelves and walls covered with handcrafts, the sum of hours and weeks and months of work. The shopkeeper demonstrated engraving techniques with the use of a wood mallet and a small simple metal pattern which could be tapped against the flat bronze to create uniform designs. There was also a row of small metal chisels to be used for freehand work. He demonstrated the different types of brass by having us hold two different sheets of metal identical in size so we could feel the change in weight.

Time seemed to lose meaning, there were no windows in the shop and we poured over all the wares until our guide showed up again. He stood in the doorway and frowned to see us still hovering over an endless variety of glowing metal plates and gave an impatient wave. “Come, we have much to see. We run out of time, come, come.”

We wound back through the streets again until we were in the midst of the Souk Dabbaghin, the tanneries quarter. We passed shop after shop stacked with piles of stretched skins. The gutters beneath our feet ran with dyed water, and the air was sharp with the scent of pigeon dung and urine which were used in the curing process. We followed our guide into a nondescript building and as we entered were handed handfuls of mint leaves which the shopkeeper plucked from a number of potted plants sitting in the foyer. From their gestures I understood that they were to be crushed and held to our nose to assist in alleviating the strong smell.

We walked up three flights of narrow spiraling stairs to an open air rooftop shop packed with finished leather goods. In the corner a man sat cross legged rubbing a stain onto a large leather purse and behind him the horizon soared with the roofs of buildings and minaret towers. Looking down at a series of connected inner courtyards I could see a honeycomb nest of large vats filled with different dyes and above, the surrounding rooftops were covered with stretched skins drying in the sun. Traditionally the dyes were vegetable in base but more and more they were being replaced by chemical dyes which were less likely to fade.

The walls of the shop were lined with traditional pointy toed leather slippers, while purses and bags hung like wind chimes from the ceiling and stacked in tidy symmetrical columns were round leather stools. The shopkeeper quickly tugged a leather jacket onto Adrian before he could protest and demonstrated how holding an open flame under the sleeve did not discolor the leather nor did spraying the sleeve with water and scrubbing it. Seeing where this line of information was headed we left the shop quickly, surprising our guide who stood in the street chatting with some friends. He gamely took us through a different maze of narrow winding gloomy alleys.

“This way here, it does not seem so much to you, very simple, very plain but behind these doors,” he gestured at the unadorned faceless panels of wood that we passed, “are very grand houses, traditional. These houses are called Riads, they are built around a large courtyard with a fountain. In summer the family lives on the first floor because the fountain makes the rooms cool, and they escape the heat. In the winter they close the lower floor off and live on the upper floors, nearer to the sun, because the heat stays above. Yes? You understand? I am taking you now to a shop in one of these Riads.”

We left the main path and veered into another series of dank gloomy walkways until we ducked through a low door and emerged into a four story high, covered courtyard. Mounted lights lit up huge antique rugs which hung down like tapestries, the floors and walls were covered with tiled mosaics and lined with carved cushioned benches and small tables which were draped with hand-woven wool throws. Stacked along the walls in adjoining rooms in deep burnt reds, dusty sand colored golds and smoky blues were an infinite variety of handmade rugs.

I felt a simultaneous thrill and crawl of fear when I realized we had entered the lion's den. Of all persuasive salesmen in the world, the ones my guidebook had warned the most about were the Moroccan rug salesmen. They were impossible to resist and the sales pitch itself could not be beaten in eloquence by a Shakespearean sonnet. We were led up four flights of winding stairs to the roof where huge looms were set up and women stood weaving and knotting. As we returned downstairs he told us that they had Berber, Persian, and Arab styles of rugs, some were loose weave while others were tight. He pulled out a finger full of wool from a rug he considered poorer quality and loose weave. The higher quality rugs were double sided and became more valuable and beautiful with age because with washing and foot traffic the knots became tighter and the natural dyes faded prettier.

The price of the rug was decided by the number of knots per square foot, which reflected the amount of time put into it. A very finely knotted rug could have more than 100,000 knots in 108 square feet of carpeting. The wool was imported from Australia and the colors were created using natural dyes. The colors of cream and brown were taken directly from the natural color of the sheep while yellow dye was traditionally made from saffron, red from poppies and pomegranates, blue from indigo, green from mint, and black from antimony.

With a snap of his fingers he had three assistants roll out rugs while another man rushed forward with a worked silver tray bearing small clear glasses of tea thick with fresh crushed mint leaves. The glasses were very small, only slightly larger than a shot glass and the contents, at first sip, were completely different from any kind of tea I had ever had. I had never been very fond of tea; I couldn't understand why a person would drink tea when they could have water instead, unless they were sick with a cold. This tea however was in a world of its own, the taste was so mouthwateringly fresh and sweet and I was so tired and thirsty that I closed my eyes just to savor the sensation of it on my tongue.

"This is amazing," I said.

"You like it? Some more?" He gave an impatient gesture at one of his assistants who disappeared before I could protest. He smiled with an air of close confidence and his eyes gleamed, "You must be careful of this tea. It tastes very good, yes? Very nice, but it is dangerous this tea. It is an aphrodisiac, look at me! I have five children!" he erupted into laughter. I frowned and put my glass down as Adrian made an amused noise next to me.

"Now, come, come, take off the shoes." He gestured at his bare feet, "Come my friends, you must walk across this rug with the bare feet to understand its texture, very nice, come, walk across."

I winced as I slowly took off my shoes and was hit by the smell. I had taken a shower just that morning but... I eyed the deep cobalt blue of the rug lined with a mosaic of white, indigo and smaller flashes of light cerulean set like jewels along the border. The salesman walked slowly back and forth across it with his bare feet and frowned when he saw us hesitate. "Come, come, you must feel with your own skin, do not worry, the oils of the feet are good for the rug, make the rug more valuable. That rug hanging there, very valuable because it is very old, many people have walked on that rug. This rug I stand on is new, not worth as much, come!"

I stepped reluctantly onto the border of the rug and when I looked up was grateful to find myself ignored. The full brunt of the sales pitch was to be directed at Adrian, who I knew to have no intention of buying. The salesman was undeterred, "You look, just look and if you see something you like you nod. If not like, then this gesture!" He made an arrogant dismissive wave with his chin high and eyes averted, as though the very sight of the rug in question was deeply offensive to him. I could see Adrian struggling not to smile.

"Come, we are friends, you just look, and later you like something we talk price. This is a good place, your money goes to those women who struggle to feed their families, prices very fair, fixed by the government. May I be followed by ill luck the rest of my days if I deceive you!" The last was punctuated with an all-encompassing gesture which seemed to call down the wrath of the heavens. I felt rather suitably impressed but Adrian looked skeptical as an avalanche of rugs began to be laid at his feet.

I wandered into an adjoining room, looking for a small rug for my mother and was followed by a silent non-English speaking assistant who pulled down the rugs I pointed to. From the adjoining room I heard, "I have five children, would I lie to you? Okay, okay for you maybe I make one time deal, friend price, family price. Come, you like this rug? You must live now! When will you come back to Morocco? Yes, maybe never come back! This rug is special my friend..."

I frowned as I made my selection with a nod; this was starting to sound serious. My rug was hardly larger than a prayer rug but was still several hundred dollars. As I walked back into the main courtyard I could see the rug in front of Adrian, who stood shaking his head, was far larger and his favorite color: a deep blue the color of the sky at twilight just after the sun had escaped the horizon but before the first evening stars.

"No problem, you did not come to buy, I understand, no bad feelings. Come, just shake my hand, brother to brother, gesture of friendship, come." Adrian looked cautious and reached his hand forward slowly as though he anticipated the ruthless bite of a viper but his sense of courtesy seemed to be overcoming his usual instincts of self-preservation.

The salesman darted his hand forward and clutched Adrian's hand firmly as though the world were ending and it was the last stable object in the world. His face filled with triumph, "Ha! Sold!" I almost expected a thunderclap from overhead to accompany this announcement and I could sense the agonized screams of Adrian's credit card.

"Whoa, no, no no no," Adrian stepped back eyes wide.

The merchant cried, "What? You try to jerk me around? Okay Ali Baba, what is your price?" Ali Baba and the forty thieves was a well-known tale in Arab countries and to call someone Ali Baba was to label them the greatest of scoundrels.

So much for fixed prices, I thought to myself, it was time to make myself scarce. I could see from Adrian's lowering brow and the merchant's howls that things could potentially get ugly. As I walked toward the main office to pay for the simple throw rug I had selected I had no idea how I was going to fit it into my already full camping backpack. I had cut down on my luggage compared to my Mexico trip but still found myself stuck with two bags and I desperately wanted to keep them from getting too heavy. A man took my rug and rolled it as small and tight as it would go before sewing a waterproof outer layer around it for easy packing. Adrian emerged through the doorway and after darting a quick look at his set face, I was almost afraid to ask.

He glanced over at me, "I got a couple rugs." I swallowed, eyes wide, and thought to myself, 'My god, a couple? Boy did this guy see us coming.' My estimation of the rug salesmen of Morocco went up a couple notches. "I wanted to get a rug in

Morocco anyways, besides he came down in price." He sounded defensive, I scowled down at my small package, I hadn't bargained thinking the prices were fixed.

Right on time our guide popped into the doorway like a jack in the box. It was a well-known fact that buying merchandise in the large cities of Fes and Marrakesh would not get you the best prices or even the best quality. Guides generally made a small commission off of whatever you bought from the store, which provided incentive for them to dump you off at their friend's shops at every opportunity. At the same time, I felt like any tour of Fes or Marrakesh that left out the shops and crafts of the merchants would be a very short tour that would miss half the culture and local flavor. There was a lot to be learned about the history and making of the handcrafts that came out of Morocco because unlike my country, most work was still done by hand following years of tradition.

Around a corner, in the climbing heat of the medina, we were led to one of the world's oldest universities and largest mosques. An old Fassi saying stated that all roads in Fes led to the Kairaouine Mosque which governed the timings of Ramadan and other Islamic festivals. It was founded in 857 AD by a wealthy Tunisian woman and could accommodate up to 20,000 people at prayer. Unclean persons, that would be us, were not allowed in but we peeked through the open door at the elaborate decorations as candle sellers around us sold decadent creations in wax to the faithful before they entered. The guide told me I could take a picture of the inside so long as I did not cross the threshold but even as Adrian frowned and shook his head I decided it wasn't a good idea.

After diving once more into the labyrinth of streets which made up the heart of the medina we stopped at Medersa el Attarine which was founded by Abu Said in 1325. It was a theological college which displayed traditional patterns of

Merenid artisanship: zellij (ceramic tilework), muquarna (plasterwork), wood carving, stucco work, and cedar wood at the top of the walls and ceilings. A medersa was known formally as a place of study but their main function was as dorms providing room and board to poor male students from the countryside and making it possible for them to attend lessons at the mosques. Most medersas in Fes remained in use up to the 1950s.

The entrance was through a stalactite domed entrance chamber which opened into a single large courtyard flanked by two sizeable halls leading into an oratory. The actual prayer hall was very bare, with a focus on its mihrab (prayer niche) flanked by marble pillars and lit by a series of small glass windows. Either side of the courtyard had stairs to the upper storey lined with student cells. In the courtyard, decoration covered every possible surface. The wood carving and joinery demonstrated the Moorish art of Laceria, "the carpentry of knots." Black Kufic script ringed three sides of the courtyard dividing the tile work from the stucco and translated to a list of properties whose incomes were given as an endowment to the medersa, rather than the usual Koranic inscriptions.

Tracing the foreign symbols on the walls with my eyes, made me feel very young, and yet in my mind it was as though the hands that carved the wood, sculpted the muquarna, and laid in the zellij were my own. Regardless of race, creed, gender weren't we all part of the pattern that the Muslims projected over and over on even the most humble of their buildings? Weren't my paintings also a form of prayer? They were a doorway I had used to step outside of myself, in order to examine my surroundings which were only a pale reflection of something vaster, greater then all of us. Something everyone and everything belonged to. In spite of wars, anger, fear, weren't we all in search of the same thing?

In the entrance hall, a circular pattern was carved into the doors and repeated in the tiling on the walls based on interlacing pentagons and five pointed stars. This demonstrated the science and philosophy employed by the craftsmen, of not representing specific ideas but rather an inner state of being. Most maalem (master craftsmen) had a single mathematical base which they worked and reworked with an unlimited number of variations on all commissions. Patterns radiating from a single point were a simile for the belief in the oneness of God as the center of every radiating pattern.

"The Bedouin could not look for God within him: he was sure that he was within God. He could not conceive anything which was or was not God, who alone was great: yet there was a homeliness, an everyday-ness of this climactic Arab God, who was their eating and their fighting and their lusting, the commonest of their thoughts, their familiar resource and companion, in a way impossible to those whose God is so wistfully veiled from them by despair of their carnal unworthiness of Him and by the decorum of formal worship. Arabs felt no incongruity in bringing God into the weaknesses and appetites of their least creditable causes. He was the most familiar of their words; and indeed we lost much eloquence when making Him the shortest and ugliest of our monosyllables."

-T. E. Lawrence The Seven Pillars of Wisdom

The Florence Academy of Art

My Dear Family, *10/11-10/17/00*

You are all probably curious to hear how school is going, I have to admit I am a little frustrated. School policy is that everyone, regardless of background, starts at the same level. So I find myself beginning where I began with Kamille years ago by copying those Xeroxes of Charles Bargue's drawings of classical Greek sculptures.

In retrospect I am not sure what I expected, I remind myself that being in Italy is an education in itself, there is so much to see. There is of course nothing wrong with starting at the beginning again. All of these exercises will serve as a refresher course which can only strengthen the technical side of my work, but it is still a blow. It is my ego that is hurt of course. I wanted to paint; I wanted to see if the painting techniques they teach here were any different from Kamille's.

The school itself is housed in a rather dreary warehouse sort of building partitioned off with curtains into small cubicle spaces often shared by up to four students and their easels. Above, skylights provide light or are covered so artificial spot lights can be used for a more dramatic light effect. It is not quite what I had imagined. I kept thinking art school in Italy: long gleaming wood floors, piano trilling softly in the background and a painter poised gracefully with a palette in hand. This is to be quite different I think, it is already extremely competitive. I am not the only one with an art background, nearly all of the first year students have art training. Some were successful art professionals and all share the goal of wanting to being the first to start painting and move over to the building which houses the advanced students.

Most students practically live at the studio and have seen little of the city and less of Italy but I can't bring myself to ignore my surroundings. I couldn't sleep this morning so I got up early to visit the Medici palace. On the way I noticed that the line at the Uffizi which normally stretches all the way around the courtyard was nonexistent and I spontaneously decided to visit. A mere twenty minutes later I was inside. Most of the exhibitions are in the upstairs galleries which open off of a main hallway filled with statues and which runs in a U shape the length of the museum. One of the rooms had some wonderful examples of Botticelli, an artist I never fully appreciated until I got to see his work in person. His paintings of the Madonna are ethereal and so detailed, the separate strands of her hair sparkle like gold.

I am reading the Agony and the Ecstasy, Irving Stone's biography of Michelangelo's life. I only have time to read before I go to bed but enjoy this book because so much of it takes place in Florence. I am constantly rounding a corner or sitting in a small piazza expecting any moment to see a ghostly vision of a young Michelangelo dreamily walking by. I went to the Medici palace, excited to see in person the Tomb of Giuliano de Medici, the Duke of Nemours, which was covered with Michelangelo's sculptures and described quite eloquently in the book. If I wasn't an artist it would be wonderful to be a rich patron who could commission such work from a master.

For the most part I love Italy, except today when a bird crapped on my jacket while I was walking to school, and then ten minutes later I stepped in fresh dog poop. We could solve world hunger if we killed the pigeons here, and shipped them to the hungry. After all, the Etruscans ate pigeons. I got nailed by a pigeon last week too, and that one had really been storing it up because it got on my sketch pad, my sweater, my hair and all over the ground. Thank god I was almost home.

Class is hard work, but I am holding my own. The models we get are inspiring. I was drawing a black girl today, she stands completely still and holds her perfectly shaped head up as though she were a queen. To me her beauty is more than the lines of her body, or exotic structure of her face. It is in that elegant poise she maintains, as though she does not experience weariness or pain. As though she were Cleopatra aware of the effect she has on others yet above it, royalty, a goddess, not life but legend.

She is from Spain and her brother poses for our sculpture class. The sculpture is a portrait so one moment I will be squinting and trying to figure out the exact contour of his nose and the next moment make eye contact with his wonderfully expressive eyes and become flustered and completely distracted.

I got my first compliment from the head instructor at school today and any compliment is a huge thing because they don't really believe in giving them. She came by to critique my drawing which was a copy of an advanced academic Bargue drawing, quite difficult and I had slaved over it for a week. She stared at it for a long time looking for mistakes. I wasn't even breathing. Finally she glanced at me and said, "Well, it is obvious you have an excellent knowledge of shading and modeling the figure. You have done a good job on that in this drawing and it is a very strong quality in your drawing skills." Of course I am passing out from shock at this time. Then she said, "But, you still need to work on your main points, seeing the basic shapes and your overall drawing under the detail."

Still, there were hardly any corrections to be made and I am almost in the lead over the other beginning students. Even though, as they keep repeating to us, it is not about the time it takes but how well and correctly you learn the techniques of drawing. Still, that was the day I was pooped on, and stepped in poop, which I am told brings good fortune and that is how I got my one and possibly only compliment. I haven't heard anyone else get such praise, so I am temporarily sitting in glory.

I was walking home with one of my roommates and saw an Arno River rat the other day. It was the size of a small cat and was swimming across the Arno, harassing the ducks, and yes, it was a rat, it had a long ropey tail. My landlord had warned us that there were huge rats that liked to swim in the Arno, but I had no idea they were that big.

My landlord took me and the roommates out for pizza which was fun except I got stuck at the end of the table with all of his Italian friends who don't speak English and my landlord thinks for some weird reason that I speak Italian very well. Maybe it is because I always make an effort, so I was forced to nod and say "Si," for three hours which was how long dinner took (my vocabulary ran out after three sentences). Oh well, I suppose it was good for me. My roommates drank a bunch of beer and accidently spilled red wine all over the table. My whole half of the table smoked, of course, and it became rather excruciating after awhile. Then for dessert, I couldn't decide between the tiramisu and cheesecake, I asked the waiter which was best, just to be polite, and he decided to flirt with me and said I must have both. Then he disappeared before I could pound him over the head. Sure enough two desserts arrived and of course of the other eight people at the table, only my landlord could be persuaded to take a few bites. I had only ordered dessert because he had said he would share one with me.

* * *

Victory today! At school, in my room of students, I am now the first one to be allowed to use charcoal, everything up to this point has only been in lead pencil. I barely beat out the stuffy British student who was a professional illustrator, and he has been coming in on weekends to work on his class projects. In sculpture class we are sculpting the skull and I am doing very well on it because of the anatomy class I took in California. We have an anatomy class here on Monday nights and unfortunately the Italian anatomy professor is still learning English. He points at slides a lot and pauses, searching for the words, then gives up and goes on to the next one. Or he will point at something, wrinkle his brow and we'll be like, "rib cage." He will be like, "raybe caahge?" We chorus, "riibbb caaaage." Anyway, mostly a very boring one hour slide show that is a lot of review for me and I generally sleep through it. After the slide show we have a nude model that he points out various muscle groups on and poses the model in a flexing, contorted position that we sketch for an hour.

The art history lectures Friday night are also accompanied by a slide show but last longer and are generally more interesting. The instructor does speak English and has published several books, one about the painter Gerome which I just finished reading. I love that artist because he traveled the world and his paintings portray atmospheric desert scenes, marble bath houses, or one was set in Rome in the old coliseum at its height with a gladiator gesturing imperiously at a roaring crowd. Last week however, the slide machine broke and the director of the school had to push each slide separately through by hand. He had to stand the whole time, so to see the slide I had to stand up and lean to the right. Plus it was a guest lecturer because the normal guy was out of town. He was Greek and if you asked him about a slide like, "who painted this?" or "where was this painted?" he'd say "I don't know," or mutter something unintelligible. Maybe he was shy.

I miss all of you, more later.

Chapter 3

Marrakesh and The High Atlas Mountains: From Snakes to Sand Dunes

"The soul of Arabia, the thunder of the Saracens
and the air of the desert came together
in the passion of the mullah's voice.
No God could ignore such a sound:
Allahu Akbar, Allahu Akbar"
–Ranulph Fiennes, Atlantis of the Sands

9/6/07

I closed my eyes and took a sip of my first cup of coffee in Morocco; it was thick, strong and accompanied by a plate of fresh croissants with honey glazed crusts. Overhead the news rattled off in a stream of Arabic accompanied by brief images, incomprehensible, indecipherable snapshots, video clips that flickered down on the voluptuously padded chairs of the hotel café. Our pocketbooks felt considerably lighter and we sat slightly subdued as we ate breakfast like two who had awoken from a deep sleep stained by dreams, a little weary, a little surprised.

Later when I swung my pack up onto my shoulders for the walk to the train station I could feel the increased weight and mourned. It seemed if I did not bring a heavy pack I was destined to fill it with heavy purchases. I could not escape the magnetic pull of my own need for belongings.

The ride to Marrakesh was a predicted nine hours and as I settled into my first class seat I had to admit to myself, some luxuries were worth the cost. I was pleased to discover that the first class car even had a bathroom with a western style toilet, toilet paper, and sink with running water. Of course the toilet did not flush and within an hour of use the sink jammed and would not turn off, spraying water in all directions. All of the toilet paper disappeared and the bathroom became quite smelly, damp, and unusable. Still, an effort at comfort had been made and even remembering second class made me shudder.

The train ride was to be our longest of the trip and I was looking forward to getting a chance to see a little more of the land between cities. As the hours crept by however, and the miles unfurled beneath the tracks, it changed very little. The scenery was arid, golden, and flat. "It looks like Mosul," Adrian said after awhile almost to himself. Then with a glance at me he added, "Iraq. Mosul was the town I was stationed in before Baghdad."

A snack cart rattled up, stocked with yogurt drinks, dry chicken sandwiches, chips, juice, soda, and, as I took an experimental sip, surprisingly good coffee, with hot milk and sugar. Eight hours later however, I had exhausted the snack cart selections, any information fellow passengers had on Marrakesh, and my interest in the emptiness of the passing horizon. As I adjusted my legs for the millionth time and struggled not to compete with Adrian for leg room I noticed with relief that we had begun to enter the outskirts of a great city. I realized we were to arrive nearly an hour earlier than I had anticipated.

Marrakesh had Berber, rather than Arab origins, in contrast to Fes and it was founded around 1060 by Youssef Bin Tachfine, a military leader who had conquered northern Morocco within two years. In 1126 the first 7km stretch of its walls were raised and constructed of tabia, red mud from the plains that had been mixed with lime. The old walled city of Marrakesh, the medina, had been named a World Heritage site which paid tribute to the history and architecture, especially the grand entrance gates, ancient mosques, and the surrounding walls.

A Moroccan man on the train had referred us to a hotel but when we found a taxi we became confused trying to repeat the foreign name which sounded like a lot of other hotel names. The taxi driver, who didn't speak any English, had no idea what hotel we were talking about, and without a word decided to drop us off downtown in front of a random hotel. We figured one hotel should be much like any other because it was still centrally located inside the medina so we gathered our luggage and went inside.

The lobby seemed promising with the requisite carved ceiling and tourist paintings depicting men on horseback in flowing robes. There were quite a few Moroccan men sitting in the lobby chairs, a few reading the paper, but I could feel their eyes boring into us as we entered. We paid fifty dollars for a room then carried our bags up several flights of stairs to the rooftop. When we stepped inside the room there was an immediate sense of barely dispelled dreariness and gloom. A single sagging bed sat rumpled in the middle with a forlorn discarded air, though I noticed the necessary TV was present, and the adjoining bathroom looked fairly clean on first glance. I had stayed in worse I figured as I gratefully took off my pack.

"This door has been broken down before." I looked up to see Adrian standing by the open door scowling at the splintered jam. He walked back outside and looked at the other doors that went off the passageway. "They all look as though they have been broken into at some point in the past. Look, this room is on the roof. It would be real easy for someone to break in while we were gone and nobody be the wiser. I don't like this, it doesn't feel safe."

I sighed, "But I'm tired. I don't know where else we can go, you don't like the places in the book and I just...wanted to take a shower."

"Think about it. Are you going to be able to enjoy your time here if all day you are wondering if your stuff will be there when you get back at night? Because I won't, I think we should find a different hotel."

Standing there tired and sweaty with my overloaded backpack next to my feet the last thing I wanted to do was heave it back on but after Adrian's assessment, I could see his point. I didn't like the situation however, the planner in me preferred going off the recommendations in the guidebook, which was careful to only suggest safe, clean hotels. Whereas traveling as we were, on the impulse, by randomly picking hotels off the street seemed risky.

We trudged back downstairs, got our money back, and found ourselves back out in the street enveloped in the glare of the sun, and weighed down by the responsibility of our luggage. I felt lost and frustrated, as though a thousand hostile eyes were watching us speculatively. As if the longer we stood stationary the more obvious our confusion became. I felt the need to walk, to move in any direction so long as the gesture of motion at least had a sense of purpose even if it was ultimately aimless. I swiveled on my heels and looked in all directions for anything that would shout out, 'haven,' anything that gave off even the whiff of comfort and the familiar.

"Look," I pointed, "Hotel. That sign over there. Come on." I darted into traffic.

"Damn it, wait," Adrian snarled behind me.

There was no time to show fear or hesitation. The road before me was an unending, howling stream of speeding taxis, buses, scooters, overloaded trucks, and darting pedestrians, all racing about in seemingly different directions. There was no order to it and not a traffic light to be seen. I gritted my teeth and dove into the ocean, feeling the steaming heat of the chaos enclose me like the furious rush of an oncoming tide and emerged panting on the other side, whole, intact.

"Don't do that! You can't... don't," he struggled for breath as he caught up, "you can't go running off like that. We have to discuss things first."

"What is there to discuss? Its roasting hot and there is a hotel sign." I set off down the road and I could hear him swear behind me.

"Sir? Madame? You want hotel? Nice clean hotel? Sir? Sir!"

In spite of myself I hesitated, we were so close to the sign, it was only a block away, though it was not the most promising looking sign. In fact the closer we got, the older and more dilapidated it was starting to look. Meanwhile a young man was following us with a look of eager impatience, waving a flyer in the air. The book had warned against the street touts advertising hotels that were quite expensive when they tacked the tout's commission onto the fee for your room. I felt a trickle of sweat run down my neck and looked at Adrian's set expression. 'Oh, the hell with the book,' I thought to myself, 'how much good had it done so far?'

"Very nice, clean, look, here is a picture of the hotel. See, cheap only thirty dollars two people."

I scowled and turned around slowly, Adrian had stopped as well. "The room has AC, TV, bathroom and its thirty dollars, for both of us?"

"Yes, yes you follow me, this way, not far." He turned and headed back the direction we had come from. I wondered what his definition of not far was. I could feel the straps of my pack biting into the flesh of my shoulders and my entire shirt was turning into a sweat soaked rag. Adrian and I exchanged a look then started after him, re-crossing the busy street, skirting past the disappointing hotel and plunging into an alley which was torn up by construction and full of gaping holes that were not even blocked off. I felt myself trip on a loose piece of concrete and moaned inwardly, where was he taking us?

He disappeared into the doorway of an unassuming building sandwiched between two small grocery shops. When we walked in we realized the hotel was a converted Riad. I could hear parakeets singing and the gurgle of a nearby fountain. As Adrian walked up to the desk and began negotiations I looked around. Every square inch of exposed walls, ceilings, and doors were covered with painted geometric patterns, elaborate tile work and like some sort of sign, prints of famous paintings by Jean Leon Gerome. I decided I didn't care what the room looked like, I liked the place. The prints on the walls were enough to earn my instant loyalty.

Thankfully the room was just as promised but as an added bonus had bars on the courtyard facing window and a strong lock on the door, so even Adrian was content. Later we discovered the roof had a panoramic terrace with views of the seventy meter tall minaret tower of the Koutoubia Mosque, one of Marrakesh's most famous monuments.

The sun had already set as we approached the central square, Djemaa El Fna in search of dinner. We followed the sound of drums and the glow of the sky which was lit up by a web of crisscrossing strings of lights, their blaze reflecting off the steam and smoke which unfurled from the cooking fires of rows of food stalls. The usual translation of Djemaa el Fna was "assembly of the dead" which referred to the public display of the heads of rebels and criminals because the square had been a place of execution up until the last century. It was an open air space in the heart of the city where people came not only to shop but also to watch a colorful montage of snake charmers, dancers, musicians, storytellers, herbalists, fortune tellers, and water sellers.

The streets were choked with people and as we began to cross to the square motorbikes and scooters careened through them with no flagging of speed. Dense crowds circled around dancing or music playing street performers. Nearly swallowed by the darkness, palm readers and fortune tellers sat alone, cross legged on the pavement in an attitude of great patience, awaiting the next customer. Male herbalists held groups of male clients captive by a sales spiel conducted in a singsong chant at full volume, while pointing to a doctor's medical dummy at various organs to illustrate key points. Spread at their feet were blankets laden with everything from the traditional stacks of horns, bones, ostrich eggs, rocks, crystals, seeds, powders, and roots to more modern plastic items like a packaged penis enlarger. The apothecary stalls also sold herbal and animal ingredients for spell binding, as well as roots and tablets for aphrodisiacs because black and white magic were still very much a part of the local culture.

Behind the square, the bazaar of Marrakesh was in full swing, it was the largest most elaborate market in all of Morocco. The maze of it hypnotized and beckoned. It seemed to hold all the mystique and eastern promise I had ever dreamed of and once lost in its hungry clutches I could imagine it would be difficult to reemerge from its walkways which were old shadowed veils of time. I didn't want to see it tired and hungry, so we tiptoed on the fringes, trying to look while not looking, careful not to step over an invisible boundary that might cause us to be sucked in. I had another mission. I was in search of the elusive snake charmers but though I saw every other sort of entertainment, the beat of the drum, the shake of a gilded belt of coins, the hip thrust of a masked dancer, there were no slithering reptiles emerging out of the gloom.

Correctly interpreting my downcast expression Adrian said, "We'll find them tomorrow, we'll return first thing. Now come on, I saw a sandwich place somewhere back there."

We passed the bright hard glitter of tourist restaurants, with their handwritten signs boasting tourist menus in a flourish of uncertain English. Live music trickled out of the entrances and curled under the nose like a chemical fragrance but we decided on a small florescent alcove that boasted quick hot sandwiches and no seating. We stood on the street against a wall, watching the sway of the crowd around us, letting the electric hum of their thoughts and small transactions brush against our skin then past us.

"Baksheesh?" A little boy stood before Adrian, his bright dark eyes fixed up on him, small hand outstretched in an age old, culture spanning gesture.

"Laa," Adrian said, his face became blank and cold as he gave a firm gesture of dismissal. The boy moved closer yet, insistent in his request. A few curt words in Arabic from Adrian and the boy's face settled into bitter lines as he spit at our feet and walked off. His form melted into the crowd so swiftly it was as though he had never been before us at all and I looked down at my half eaten sandwich in dismay, wondering if he had been hungry.

"Don't ever hand out money on the street." I looked up at Adrian's voice. "In Iraq the boys worked in teams. One would come up to a soldier begging for change and the other boys would be watching to see where the money was kept. Then they would swarm the soldier in a group, one pick-pocketing him while the others distracted him. I knew quite a few Joes who lost their wallets that way."

I sighed and shifted in place, "Yeah... but..."

"Trust me, you think nobody is watching us right now? You aren't helping these kids by giving them money, you're just encouraging them to beg and to steal." Adrian turned looking for a trash can as he wadded up his empty sandwich wrapper.

"Did anyone ever try to pick your pocket?" I asked.

"One kid, just one. I caught him at it though and grabbed him by the arm before he could take off. I marched him down to the police office where I knew the chief and told him I had caught Ali Baba trying to pick my pocket," Adrian shook his head, a reluctant look of amusement crossing his face. "The chief told the kid I was like a brother to him and stealing from me was equal to stealing from him and that the punishment was to be lined up and shot out back."

"Oh my God!" I burst out.

"Oh give me a break, I love kids. You think I would have some little kid get shot for trying to pick my pocket? The point was to teach the kid something. To get him to stop before something bad happened. The chief told the kid that the only reason he wasn't going to be shot for his offense was that I had interceded on his behalf but that if it ever happened again... Every time the kid saw me after that on the street he would wave and call out, 'Sadeeq! Sadeeq!'" At my look of incomprehension Adrian said, "Friend, 'sadeeq' means friend. Nobody ever tried to pick my pocket after that. Word must have gotten out."

As we started to walk back I tried to make sense of it: patrolling the streets, waiting for gunshots, always listening for explosions. Every innocuous seeming pile of trash on the street corner was a potential homemade bomb, and even a small child begging for change could be more than he seemed. Of the two of us, Adrian had always been more patient and compassionate when it came to children. He wanted some of his own one day, whereas I had never had any interest in having a family. It was instinctive, to want to give when someone asked, especially to a child, a being weaker, smaller than myself, but was an instant of generosity, a few dollars, helpful in the long run? Did it change a life, or did it just serve to feed a mentality of expectation?

As I wove through the crowd I noticed a small stir at a nearby street café where a white, female tourist had sat down at a café with all male clientele. Our guide in Fes had warned us that the cafes on the street were only for men and it was considered very vulgar for a woman to sit down at one. Outdoor street seating made cafes desirable places to stop and drink coffee and tea and all the more deceptive to the taboo female. It served to remind me once again, that I was not in Europe. I was an ocean away from the United States and the rules were completely different. I wondered if she would be served or asked to leave.

* * *

The next morning after breakfast in our hotel courtyard, we walked back to the main square. It seemed quieter, the food stalls had been replaced by a ring of carts stacked with glowing oranges and we each had a glass of freshly squeezed orange juice. I tilted my face up to the sun and closed my eyes to savor it, the flavor, the scents, the sounds. Then I heard it. Turning I saw a circle of men standing around a temporarily pitched tent that shaded a small portion of flagstones. I could hear the soft low impact of the drums and the rising sinuous notes of the oboe-like ghaitahs. My breath caught as I started forward.

The backs of the crowd blocked my view and I had a momentary impulse to crouch down and peek through their legs. Finally, behind a shoulder, around a head, and I raised up on my tiptoes and rocked forward to catch a glimpse. A cluster of Aissaoua musicians sat in a semi-circle, in front of them laid hand drums flush to the pavement. Even as I watched, one was lifted to reveal the still coils of a black cobra, which quivered slightly before writhing outwards, tentative, experimenting, then inquisitive, exploring.

A turbaned man, not much older than a boy sat back on his haunches and his voice rose and fell, soft and nasal, to combine and merge with the musicians until I could not tell where he began and the ghaitah took over. In a single fluid motion he reached forward and picked the cobra up by its middle. I had a flash then, of the bull rushing the matador, the dance, the play, as though the lack of fear was all that kept the matador from dying in the ring. The crowd did not breathe and he held the snake up, as though speaking to it, whispering a tale of the desert and the sun and the cool of the rock to shelter from the heat. A whisper of the old world, old tunes, old patterns, the tale of the prey rustling in the dark. The hood flared, and the small vicious head reared back, but only to sway back and forth mirroring the movement of the singer. A movement that seemed to speak of wind, the gesture of the breeze, a breath of day followed by night and the stars that watched from the sky. It was difficult to tell who was mesmerizing who.

Robed men walked through the crowd with young desert rattlers looped around their necks offering them to tourists to have their pictures taken with. Adrian was told not to worry as they deposited one around his neck. The snakes had had their venom drained recently but if he was to get bitten he should try to get bitten on the hand as opposed to the face or neck so if there was any residual venom it would give them more time to be able to help him. "Great," Adrian muttered as he handed the man his camera.

I left the snake charmers reluctantly and we went to stand before the entrance to the bazaar, an innocuous looking shaded passageway speckled with flower spots of sun that fluttered down from gaps in the overhead canopies. I reminded myself not to buy anything. It was not so much a question of money but of how much I wished to carry. I must consider the bite of the straps into my shoulders, the pull of the bag I rolled behind me. I must think ahead.

We had been of one mind in deciding to make the day's venture without a guide, we needed no encouragement when it came to purchases. Plunging in we discovered that the prices of items were so inflated that the best thing to do was to find several things you were looking for at the same stall, take the price provided and deduct about 75% then start negotiating from there. Often a whole series of stalls would be family related and when done with one, we would quickly be passed on to the next family member who sold wood work, then the next who sold scarves.

I was drawn to a closed antique store by a wall of paintings that I stood looking at until the adjoining rug salesman said he had just the store for us. He led us through a maze of alleys, telling us that this store was special. It was a wholesale artisans store with only the finest quality items and to gain entrance one had to know the precise location because it was hidden in the maze. On the way we paused at an innocent looking enclosed courtyard that he pointed out to us. It was La Criee Berbere, a small square that was the site of the old slave auctions which used to be held before sunset every Wednesday, Thursday, and Friday until 1912.

After awhile, I could tell by Adrian's face he was beginning to wonder what we had agreed to as our journey stretched and lengthened. Yet, we didn't leave the bazaar, we simply went deeper and deeper, until I had lost all sense of direction and had no idea of how we would find our way back out. We finally entered a small innocuous alley and watched our guide pause before an unlabeled door and knock. Adrian and I exchanged looks. Before our experiences with the market of Fes we would have been nervous but the carefully cultivated mystique of these hard to find shops was becoming more commonplace to us. Still, even as we waited for the door to be opened I could not help but feel as though we stood before the door of an old fashioned speakeasy, about to gain entrance into the Moroccan underworld.

After a few words with the man who opened the door we were passed off to an English speaking salesman who ushered us into a large two story high shop with the air of one who was conferring a great favor. Every square inch of wall and available space was choked with merchandise: brass Djinni lanterns caught the light, shelves of silver jewelry glowed in glass cases, antique knives made from horn and bone hung from leather looped sheathes, multi-paned glass lamps dangled from the ceiling and vases perched on pedestals in the center of the room.

"My friends, you look, if you like something you tell anyone and it will be placed on this table here. When you are finished with looking you come and sit and we shall have tea and speak about price. There is no pressure here. You do not buy, no problem. You do not like the price you do not have to buy. My friends, I am a man of my word. When you leave this store whether you have purchased something or not, we will remain friends, no bad feelings. Please enjoy."

Looking around I realized nothing in the store had a price tag, a very ominous sign I decided. After 45 minutes of looking we decided to play the game and sat down on low stools with two antique knives and two silver bracelets on the wood table before us. I could not help but feel a quiver of nervousness as the small glasses of hot tea were brought out and presented to us. After a few moments, when the salesman had decided that the relaxing and euphoric quality of the tea must have taken effect, he gently mentioned a price in the thousands of euro. I sat for a moment stupefied in shock, the level of which was so great that it was the only thing that kept me from careening out the door. There was simply an inability at first to fully comprehend the price. When I realized Adrian was not getting up, I gulped down the rest of my tea and asked for another. I decided watching my travel companion spend this much money was going to need more relaxation then one cup could provide.

When the salesman got up to order the tea, I leaned over to Adrian and hissed, "Aren't you paying attention? He said 3,500 euro not 350. Are you insane? Its...they're... just some dumb knives for god's sake."

Adrian choked on his tea and whispered back, "Are you sure, I thought he said..."

"No, no, god let's get out of here, this is going to be worse than the rug seller. Come on, I will get up first-," I broke off as the salesman sat back down with a smile and I held my breath waiting for a signal from my companion which did not come. The tea was refilled, a knife subtracted, and the price began to be thrown back and forth in a leisurely sort of fashion. I felt as mesmerized as the snake in the square. Finally after Adrian had been called Ali Baba many times, the price drastically reduced, an agreement was reached. I left on shaky legs, still unsure of what had happened but positive of at least one thing, light headed, I desperately needed something to eat.

Back in the alleyway I looked from one way to the other, yet all of the shops and small branching footpaths seemed the same, I was not even sure of which direction to set off in. "Djemaa el Fna?" I asked an amused shopkeeper who pointed past his stall. Adrian was silent behind me and I wondered if the reality of his purchases had sunk in yet. Though our budgets were different, his living situation was similar to mine. His belongings were in a permanent state of limbo, at times unpacked or partially revealed in half open boxes which took up space in a temporary apartment. They were always eventually repacked and shoveled into storage. It was difficult for me to purchase anything that would not be given as a gift, though Morocco was unlimited temptation. I could easily fill an apartment with their hand-carved wood furniture, hammered metal framed mirrors, dangling glass lanterns, and falling shrouds of colored silk.

My stomach made a low protest as I walked and I could feel myself getting dizzy, still my feet slowed then stopped in front of an art gallery. Unstretched canvas was tacked carelessly on the open doors and crowded over every surface of the interior walls. The outside light reflected off the glare of oil before being absorbed to reveal glimpses of the faces and figures of Moroccan people.

I was starving, yet there was no way I would be able to find this shop again, deep within the labyrinth. I had passed many small tourist galleries, stuffed with stacks of badly painted desert scenes and luridly tinted camels marching into the sunset. These paintings had a flicker of life, a touch of spices, a form arrested in mid-gesture, a cloaked woman walking through the market place, a man crouched down in front of his wares robed in a swath of crimson cloth. For every canvas tacked to the wall there were piles of loose canvas resting on every surface. The shopkeeper was a painter of some of the abstract pieces and when Adrian showed interest in the paintings with horses he proceeded to tell us about his family who raised horses. Horses so dear they were considered children and would be sold for no price. His father would let few people even ride them. His family was very traditional, his father and mother would sit to eat and only then were the children allowed to sit and to this day his father's chair could only be sat in by the head of the family which was now the oldest son, his brother. The price of the paintings was low and made even lower with each painting we added on and we found ourselves leaving with four.

"That's it, besides food we are not allowed to buy anything else today," I growled some time later as I bit into my sandwich.

"Tell me about it," Adrian sighed. "Whoa, what's this?" He stopped to examine a billboard which advertised expeditions to the Sahara desert.

"Sir? Madame? You like maybe to go to Sahara? Ride the camel, yes? Very cheap for you, special deal." Adrian stared at him and I could sense where this was going. My main desire in Morocco had been to see the snake charmers, whereas Adrian's goal had always been to ride a camel into the Sahara desert. So much for not buying anything else today, I thought to myself as we followed the man to an office a block away and signed up for a discounted three day expedition that left very early the next morning.

* * *

"No," I moaned as the alarm went off and I struggled out of the sheets. I knew there would be no time for breakfast and coffee as I quickly got my things together and dressed. We stored the bulk of our bags with the hotel and made our way to the appointed meeting spot.

As we waited on the sidewalk, more and more tourists began to arrive, identifiable not necessarily by race or dress but because of the large camping backpacks on each one's back that seemed to match the ones both Adrian and I sported. They stood uneasily in pairs on the appointed sidewalk where we were to be picked up by the tour van. When their number reached over twenty, Adrian and I started to look with concern at each approaching minibus. I began to envision a hellish ride crammed shoulder to elbow to armpit with luggage haphazardly stacked on the roof, the odd piece coming loose and falling unnoticed into the ditch as we jounced along over potholes. The low cost of the expedition started to seem like less of a happy coincidence and more like a desperate effort by the company to overstuff a ghetto tour. We were greatly relieved when two groups were peeled off and put in different vehicles, which left us with a more manageable group. When we were finally herded into a midsized bus it had cushioned seats, plenty of room, and space in the back for luggage.

The rest of the morning the landscape changed from city to arid flatlands until the bus began to slowly climb into the foothills of the High Atlas Mountains. The Atlas mountains are the highest mountain range in North Africa and run across Morocco from the ocean in the east to northern Algeria in the west, almost 1000km and were inhabited by the Berbers. Until the 1920s when the French began their pacification efforts, the Berber people were very isolated and their way of life had been based upon the control of three main mountain passes by a trio of clan families called “the Lords of the Atlas.” It wasn’t until 1933, and only then with the cooperation of the main feudal chief Thami el Glaoui, that the French were able to control them and their tribal land.

Traditional mountain village architecture was a mix of stone and clay houses tiered on rocky slopes, fortified agadirs (collective granaries) and Kasbahs, (feudal castles for community defense). Berber women, unlike the Arab women in the lowland cities, were unveiled and performed almost all of the heavy labor: working the fields, herding and grazing the cattle and goats, as well as carrying loads of brushwood and provisions.

We made frequent stops at panoramic lookouts, each of which had a handful of vendors selling local rocks and crystals. It was difficult to understand our driver at each stop. He spoke hardly any English and what he uttered was in a bare French whisper picked up only by the first row of seats. We were in the back.

One stop in a small dusty village seemed only a snack and bathroom break but as Adrian and I wandered down the street following a trickle of tourists, the shops abruptly ended and we came across the empty expanse of a dried up riverbed. On the other side was an old crumbling Kasbah situated on dark jagged rock. Sheer red clay walls rose against the red hills and when I relaxed my vision and let my eyes blur the walls melted into the rock and the Kasbah became invisible. Despite the lack of electricity or plumbing it was still inhabited by a handful of families who made money off the tourists, film companies, and to a limited extent, the valley's agriculture.

As we walked across the river bed, two young boys, no older than 10, fell into step with us. They spoke English as well as a smattering of at least four other languages and offered to give us a tour of the Kasbah. The Kasbah before us, called Ait Benhadou, dated from around the 16th century and the films "Gladiator" and "Lawrence of Arabia" were both shot there. Orson Welles was also known to have used it for his films, "Sodom and Gomorrah" and "Jesus of Nazareth."

I wasn't sure how long we had to explore. I could see a handful of people from our group walking far ahead of us until, in a shimmer of heat thickened air, they were swallowed up against the rising hills. The closer we came, the higher the rose tinted walls loomed before us. As we walked through the main gate it was to enter into silence thick and slumberous as though the city were not dead, only barely breathing under an opium enchantment. The boys pointed our way through dark doorways and up narrow winding stairs to vacant rooftops. The crumbling crenellated walls were a frame for the lapis stone of sky whose polished, unblemished expanse was broken only by its kiss to the horizon. Staring at the rock hills and the fortified structure of the granary far above the city, I felt a terrible impatience gnaw at my heart. The hot breath of afternoon brought a scent of dust but I craved the thick rich scent of linseed oil, the bite of turpentine. I wanted, in that moment, nothing more than to be the last person on earth, alone with my paints in the slumbering city.

"Honey? Could you come take my picture?"

"Yeah," I said as I turned back reluctantly. "Sure." I knew there would be no way to return here, short of renting a car. My guidebook had warned of the difficulties of traveling outside of a guided tour in these mountains. I needed to wait. I needed to dig up some of my hard earned patience which had got me through completing the many academic drawing studies so I could learn to paint. I needed to store my hunger for my brushes. I tried to take pictures with my mind as I resigned myself and hands clenched, returned to the van.

Later at a stop for lunch I was short with Adrian and I could sense the rigidness of my body, the stone of frustration sitting inside of me and I had to walk away. I left him with the others at the restaurant and crossed the street to lose myself in a tangle of old footpaths lined by tall clay walls. A young man watching my silent explorations stopped me and pointed me down an alley to a view that looked out over a valley. I took a deep breath as I stared at the horizon and tried to identify the source of my frustration. It wasn't only the inability to paint, it was being part of a couple, never alone with my own thoughts, not traveling at the pace I wanted to travel, staying at the sort of places I was not used to staying in. When I was with Adrian I wasn't an artist, I struggled even to see as one, to think like one. Instead my time was spent shopping for souvenirs I didn't need as I fought to remember who I was, the person separate from Adrian. What we wanted out of life was so dissimilar, yet I loved him. I was afraid to be without him and our remaining time together was so short. I forced myself to let it go, I couldn't take my stress out on him. I needed to appreciate what I had for as long as I was allowed to have it. I returned penitent and not finding Adrian waiting by the van with the others I followed my instincts and aimed my feet toward a collection of shops.

"Madame? You like to see something? My shop is over here."

"Actually I am looking for someone," I paused, beginning to smile. "A man... Ali Baba?"

"Ah yes, he is over here, my friend's shop."

Peering around the corner I found him surrounded by a collection of wares the store keeper kept adding to, perched on a low stool with a cup of tea in hand. "Hey... I'm sorry," I said.

Adrian got up with a smile, "I think you should get me out of here."

"Yeah," I said, "let's go."

Hurtling along in the minivan for hours our group became less a cluster of suspicious strangers and began to coalesce into distinct personalities. There were three disheveled young Japanese students traveling together, a couple from Spain who sat next to me that I was able to chat with quite well in Spanish. There was a man from Scotland and his wife from the U.K., a man traveling alone from Columbia, another lone man with a head of white blonde hair from Austria, and a couple from Italy.

The reds melted out of the rock and were replaced by dusty ochres as we entered the Dades Gorge. When the sun began to set we were still rattling at breakneck speeds past groups of rock formations burned a blazing orange gold by the late sun. The bottoms of the gorges were a lush green, covered with carefully tended fields of fig and pomegranate trees, brussel sprouts, alfalfa, and corn.

That night we stayed in the Dades Gorge at an isolated hotel that was perched above a small trickling river. The hotel itself was a sprawling three stories high with colorful intricate murals painted on the lobby walls and endless rambling hallways that ended in clean and spacious rooms. Our room overlooked the river but unfortunately for Adrian, who seemed to feel it more than I, the room was quite warm without even a fan or stray breeze from the window to stir the air. I noticed there was no TV and was silently grateful, sleep that night would be flavored by the sound of moving water. Dinner was served on an open verandah and consisted of a generous spread of fresh bread, vegetable and rice soup, sautéed vegetables over couscous, tender chicken, and a dessert of sweet, ripe, honeydew melon.

* * *

I took a long swallow of coffee punctuated by a bite of my Moroccan crepe, similar to a pancake only greasier, and felt immensely peaceful and grateful. My tranquility seemed matched by my fellow travelers who looked clean and still damp from their showers. Speech over breakfast was languid and soft. It lasted until we got back into the van and drove for hours and hours until everyone was sprawled out sticky, sweaty, and rumpled. The quick break at the Dades hotel was already a distant memory. The air was permeated by engine exhaust and sighs.

We took a lunch break at the Todra Gorge where the bus vomited us out at a restaurant nearly buried under huge looming vertical red cliffs. The cliffs were so tall and massive that standing under them I could not help but feel dwarfed, almost claustrophobic, as though anything so big and tall was defying gravity. The longer I stood gazing up, the more I could not help but sense they were quivering in place. Restless in their rocky souls they desired adventure, movement; they craved chaos and destruction and wrestled against their confinement.

They were whispering promises to the air, the breeze, the roots of the small plants which held them and any minute their quiver would become a shiver, metamorphosing into a shudder, a spasm, a quake that would bring all of it howling down in a spasm of joyous freedom.

Adrian and I wandered down the road which unwound on the banks of a cool still stream that the local children swam in. In the heat, the sight of them splashing in the clear water was tempting, yet in my mind arose color photographs from National Geographic of bizarre parasites festering on hapless African tribes. It was typical American paranoia, but I stayed out of the water.

After lunch we were on the road again and our next stop some hours later was El Gififate where we were handed off to a local guide who showed us through an old Kasbah, parts of which were abandoned. He led us into my first mosque, which accepted our heathen feet only because it was abandoned; the faithful had left its echoing spaces and taken their prayers elsewhere. Sunlight licked down the walls, pillars, and archways from an opening cut in the center of the ceiling, a square opening to the eye of God. The light tumbled through, smoothing fingers over unadorned walls, breathing down the length of columns, reverberating, echoing as it spoke the name of light in a thousand different tongues. It was as though the light was alive in the effect it had on all it touched, transforming, creating, coalescing. As I stood there, I tried to imagine how it must have been filled with people, the walls ringing with the tones of voices singing their praises to the sky. Even now, in its silence, it was a space worthy of prayer. How could anyone not be touched by the divine surrounded by such an effect of color in the trembling transition from sunlight to caressing shadow?

Outside we saw women and children washing huge rolled up mats in the stream and eating from large shared plates of couscous and vegetables. The tour was invited to join in and a few did. I was told later by one of the Spanish tourists that he accidently reached with his left hand into the communal bowl of food. He did not quite realize the depth of the cultural blunder he had committed until I told him about the local bathroom habits, and the symbolism of his gesture. The poor man was horrified and I was mentally grateful that the first day in Morocco Adrian had repeatedly reminded me about not gesturing, pointing, or reaching for anything with my left hand, until it had become an unconscious habit.

At the end of the tour of the Kasbah we left the medina and wound up back in the commercial portion of town. Our tour group was sneakily left at a 'weavers,' really the shop of a Berber rug salesman, who served the requisite hot mint tea. He explained the different types of rugs as his daughter demonstrated the refining of wool and then weaving on a large stand up loom. It was mostly old news to Adrian and I, having heard much the same spiel in Fes, and I focused my eyes on my crossed legs when the informational lecture ended and the sales pitch began. When he asked if anyone would be interested in buying anything, the room echoed in silence. I snuck a peek, even the Japanese were not biting. He switched tactics and began to pick rugs to roll out on the floor, addressing individuals, his tone at once caressing, then cajoling as though he spoke to a particularly stubborn horse.

I sat aloof, amused, until he rolled out a large rug made of cactus silk, whose burnt golden saffron color arrested my eyes. His spiel was directed at a British woman who looked as though she wished she could dissolve through the floor, as though she were wondering how rude it would be to get up and walk out the door. In my mind I could see that rug on a wood floor, carelessly laid out near an easel, holding the light even as the sun began to set. A room I didn't have, a floor that did not exist and suddenly I wanted to buy that rug for myself. Buy it for the invisible nonexistent studio that I desperately wanted, a small illusory piece of permanence. I entered the fray with a swoop, to the shocked looks of those around me. Adrian stared at me as though I had grown an extra head. How many times had I counseled him not to buy another item to be saddled with? How many times had I given a sigh of exasperation with each new purchase he had made? The salesman's starting price was 1800 dirham; I suggested 1500 which he said was impossible. I looked at the rug forlornly and was secretly grateful to be spared the purchase. Then he murmured, with a look of commiseration, that perhaps he could make me a deal. The price could be lowered to 1500 if I threw in my watch.

I frowned down at the used plain item which sat so innocuously on my wrist and gave a shrug, "Sure, all right." He deftly unbuckled the watch and speedily put it on his daughter, the weaver's wrist.

"I am sending her away to school, she will use this. It is a very nice thing for her," he said looking pleased. She smiled and came forward to kiss me on both of my cheeks.

Once the weaver and his daughter's attention focused elsewhere I became aware of Adrian sitting frozen next to me staring at me in an attitude of shock. "Did you just trade the first gift I ever gave you... for a discount on a rug?" His whisper was heard by a few of the closer situated couples from the tour who turned to stare at me with a mixture of amusement and horror. I stared down at my naked wrist and began to process exactly what I had done as the packaged rug was placed by my knee.

"Oh... yeah... I guess it was you that gave me that watch." A sense of great shame blanketed me as he buried his face in his hands and shook it back and forth. "It was just a Wal-Mart watch though. I mean I was there when you got it, it wasn't even for a special occasion, it..." I trailed off as I realized that not only was I making things worse but that all of that was beside the point. "I'm sorry, I really didn't do it on purpose. I don't know what I was thinking! Damn rug salesmen anyway, it's...it's our guide's fault! How could he leave us here?"

Adrian looked across the room and sighed, "Well I guess it was worth it, his daughter looked pretty happy. They can't really get things like that here, of decent quality. Good luck trying to find a reliable replacement. Oh yeah, and don't ever, ever ask me to buy you another watch. A thousand years could go by, you could beg me on your knees and I wouldn't buy you another watch... traded for a rug... don't come crying to me when your luggage gets too heavy."

It was in this way I learned that negotiating with a Berber was vastly different from haggling with an Arab. With an Arab the price was always fluid and only ruled by the law of three. Three prices could be named but the third price would be the last offered and had to be accepted. With a Berber, the price was fixed but could be lowered or waived in light of an appropriate trade. Up for exchange was anything on your person including jewelry, cameras, clothing, or even aspirin. As fate and galactic justice would have it, I would spend the rest of my trip and even months afterward having abominable luck with watch after replacement watch.

The Berbers were the first modern people to arrive in Morocco 4,000 years ago. They developed kingdoms and came under the control of the Roman Empire around 40 A.D. The name 'Berber' originated from 'Barbarus,' a name given to the people by the Romans who considered them barbarians. In the High Atlas Mountains some Berbers called themselves 'Imazighen' which meant "free people," though they were eventually conquered by the Arabs. The Berbers made up half the population of present day Morocco and still spoke Berber, which was an unwritten oral language with culture, history, and crafts passed down through speech alone.

With the golden rug, which displayed a more modern pattern that the rug seller had playfully termed, 'Picasso,' I climbed back into the van and the tour continued on. The closer we got to Merzouga and the famous Erg Chebbi sand dunes, the flatter and more desolate the landscape became. The Erg Chebbi was Morocco's only genuine Saharan erg, an impressive drifting chain of sand dunes that could rise to more than 800 feet.

The road stretched straight ahead for miles and as we rattled along, the dust, heat, and size of insects all seemed to increase exponentially. Finally we turned off of the highway and followed a series of tire tracks. No other semblance of road was visible on the flatlands which stretched for miles to the horizon.

After 10km we drove through a stone arch into a large courtyard sided with low buildings and stone walls, behind it stretched the beginning of the Sahara. The sun was already low on the horizon and the dunes crested and rolled before us in the colors of autumn, carved out by lengthening violet shadows. The Sahara was mostly hard packed sand but about ten percent of it was covered by sand dunes. The dunes were constantly shifted by the wind which blew grains of sand off the ridges to begin a new ridge, so dunes seemed to walk across the desert. At night, because there was no plant life to hold the heat and no moisture in the ground, the temperature could easily drop 40 degrees.

Each of us was assigned a camel and given instructions to bring only what we needed for the night. I opted for water, a book and a jacket. At our last bathroom/café stop, an hour previous, we had been told there would be no water ahead and if we wanted it we needed to purchase it and bring it along because none would be provided. There had been a wild flurry of hot dusty tourists waving fistfuls of dirham at the dazed and momentarily overwhelmed man behind the café counter. In the heat and excitement of the moment we had all bought maybe too much water. Adrian packed in his backpack four large bottles for the two of us and three for the Spanish couple. His camping backpack was then so heavy he lurched from side to side like a man in the last throes of intoxication as he walked. There were no separate pack camels so despite disgusted looks from our camel guides he kept the backpack on as he got on his kneeling camel which then moaned despairingly as it struggled to stand under the weight.

The camels of Morocco had only a single hump and were called dromedaries. They were originally brought to the region almost 2,000 years ago by the Romans and served as vital links in the salt trade routes across the Sahara from Marrakesh to Timbuktu. A camel could carry a load of 400 pounds or more and could survive losing up to 25% of its body weight in water through dehydration. It had padded feet like snowshoes perfect for crossing the shifting floor of the desert. Its hump stored fat, and long lashes and heavy brows protected the eyes from blowing sand.

My camel was playfully labeled 'punk' by the Japanese students because of the ring through its nose and its spiky tuft of hair that stuck up disreputably around an irritated gaze. There was a hot dusty wind blowing through the dunes and as we lost sight of the buildings behind us, there was nothing to be seen in any direction but the undulating mountains of sand. Adrian named his camel Kerbal, and chatted with it for the two hours it took to get to camp. We agreed besides being the largest, his camel was definitely one of the handsomest of the ragtag string being in possession of a very soft, clean, approachable looking nose.

When we got to camp it was full dark, the stars had come out and were blazing in the clear sky. The desert felt timeless and I wanted to pretend I wasn't just a tourist, but a part of the desert and it a part of me. Instead as I watched the activity of the guides, I felt like a guest. A barely tolerated inconvenience who had no more comprehension of the desert then of the age of the stars that gazed down upon me.

Camp was a circle of cloth tents in the center of which the guides spread rugs and then mattresses around a single lit lantern. We sat and drank tea until dinner, which consisted of a large dish of cooked vegetables, savory broth and meat, followed by a dessert of sliced oranges. I was surprised to see small rushes of movement in the shadows, just out of the light cast by the lantern. A glitter of eyes watched us, guarding, prowling, until a low invisible meow echoed out of the night. Then it was as though their cloak of concealment was lifted and we could see them. Cats, waiting, hunting, perched on top of the tents or curled at the bases.

* * *

I woke and stared at the draping cloth above my head. The night before, crawling into the dim tent, barely lit by a single lamp that had seemed to create more shadows then it had banished I had laid on my thin, sand sprinkled mattress and envisioned scorpions, bedbugs, lice, giant desert spiders and snakes until the sum of my own paranoias had lulled me to sleep.

Adrian moaned next to me and I turned over carefully to look at him. I realized with amusement that the self-proclaimed dog person had a small white cat curled up on his feet and a pile of nearly five cats curled up on the far side of him. "What..." his eyes opened and he sat up suddenly shocking the entire mountain of sleeping cats into flight. The small cat at his feet only meowed loudly and turned over. "What time is it?"

I checked my bare wrist, "Why are you asking me?" I grumbled irritably.

He sighed and rummaging around pulled out his iPod, "5:26...in the morning... and I am wide awake... great." The cat at his feet opened one eye to glare at both of us before closing it again. I pushed back my blanket and stepped out of the tent. On first glance nobody else seemed to be up either.

"I thought I heard voices earlier," Adrian said as he stepped out behind me, an indignant yowl trailed out behind him. "Oh wait, there they are." I followed his gaze and saw silhouetted against the sky, atop the crest of an enormous sand dune, nearly our entire group. Adrian started toward them and as I followed I was surprised at how difficult it was. The sand toward the base of the dune was loose and deep, it sucked at my feet and walking through it was similar to wading through heavy snow. Midway up the sand became a little firmer, but the last six feet up to the crest the sand was very loose. The angle was nearly vertical and I had to climb up on all fours, scrambling furiously for purchase. I finally heaved myself up next to Adrian, wheezing, the muscles in my legs trembling and Adrian eyed me thoughtfully, not even out of breath.

Around us, as far as the eye could see, the Sahara stretched unbroken, dim in the predawn but slowly lightening. A wail trailed out in the direction I had come from and as I watched, the small white cat made its way up the dune having followed us from the tent. "Geez Adrian, what did you do? Feed it? You know for someone who doesn't like cats they sure like you."

Adrian's shoulders slumped as he watched the feline make its way up to us. "Damn cats," he muttered.

The rest of group sat silent, waiting. We could feel the sun before we saw it. There was a charge to the air, a taste of heat before it was glimpsed, a dryness at the back of the throat. The horizon turned silver, so bright it was without color, rippling like water over the ridges of dunes, a cascading rolling tide. It was as though we saw the glittering ripples of a vast ocean trailing before us. The light changed without sound. If I listened I could hear the whisper of my breathing and the breathing of those around me but there was no cry of birds, no distant motors of traffic, the slamming of a door. All of the ever present, familiar sounds of civilization were gone. The Sahara seemed in that moment untamable; similar to the ancient sheets of glacier ice in Alaska that moved so slowly they could not be captured with the eye, changed without changing, lived without living.

A half hour later the guides appeared below and waved us down. As we began the descent I heard whooping and hollering and we all turned to look at the same time. On an adjacent dune the two Japanese men had taken off all of their clothes and were running around completely naked while the female of their group took pictures. I shook my head but could feel the smile on my face and I wished in that moment I had the courage to do the same thing, to be naked in the sun and plunge into the ocean of light, to become drunk on it. It would have been the memory of a lifetime caught not with a flat photograph but with all of the senses.

On the camel ride back, the sun threw our shadows next to us in perfect marching silhouettes. The shapes of the dunes against the pure cobalt blue sky seemed surreal. A Dali-esque canvas that waited for the punch line, a dripping clock, a vacant door, an elongated figure silhouetted. I wished for the millionth time I could stay and paint but I couldn't see how it would work. Back at the main building we had breakfast before piling in the van and beginning the drive back to Marrakesh.

Our bus stopped for lunch in front of another overpriced restaurant and our group was immediately swarmed with menus shoved in our faces as soon as we disembarked the van. I looked across the street at the competition, an empty restaurant that did not have the connection with our driver. A waiter wiped desultorily at one empty table with an abandoned air. He glanced up at our van with a look that held a wealth of resignation.

"Let's go over there. It will be quieter, we won't have to wait as long for food and we can finally get away from the rest of the group." Adrian's eyes followed my gesture and he nodded.

We crossed the street and without consulting a menu sat down. At the first rattle of our chairs the waiter's eyes snapped open and a hopeful, anxious smile began to creep across his face.

"Hey, good idea. God, how obnoxious, just shoving menus in our faces like that." I looked up and realized the rest of the group had followed us and were busy pulling out the chairs around us. My shoulders slumped but the waiter was overjoyed. His back straightened, eyes gleamed and he became a whirlwind of activity.

Back in the van we flew through many of the areas we had stopped and lingered at on the way to the dunes. By the time we hit the mountain passes and the switchbacks I felt tired and numb as I stared down the steep drops, automatically tightening my seat belt and hoping the driver would not answer his cell phone as it went off for the third time.

We didn't get back to Marrakesh until late and were deposited unceremoniously in the middle of a busy street while the van double parked, taking up an entire lane. We emerged into a roar of noise, surrounded on all sides by a sea of cars, scooters and hurrying people. There was a flurry of activity as everyone quickly organized their belongings, strapped on backpacks, then headed in different directions without a backward glance or wave goodbye. I could feel the sand of the

Sahara stuck in my hair, lining the inside pockets of my pants and coating my ankles under my socks.

Adrian and I strode grim faced to our hotel and were quickly given a room that had a large fan which kept it cooler than the lugging AC unit of the room we had before we left. Adrian threw himself across the bed facedown, arms spread-eagled. “Don’t ask me to move because it ain’t gonna happen,” came the muffled voice.

Starving, I threw down my bag and went back out to troll the streets for food. I went to our favorite sandwich shop and got two sandwiches to go. In my weariness every face seemed strange and full of sinister intent and I was grateful when I got back to the room. As we sat watching the news in Arabic and munching on fries, I could not help but feel triumphant in the roll of provider. I could not have been prouder than had I hunted our dinner and carried it back bleeding across my shoulders.

* * *

“I think I have completely had it with the bazaar, no more markets. I am shopped out,” Adrian said as he jerked his neck to the left, then the right in an effort to pop it. I took a sip of coffee and frowned as I consulted my guidebook.

“Well, lets’ see, there is the Palace Bahia: once the residence of the Grand Vizier Ahmed ben Moussa, a very smart and cruel black ex-slave who rose to hold enormous power. Hmmmmm,” I frowned as I read on. “However, the moment the vizier died, his slaves pillaged the palace and a few days later nothing remained but the empty building. His family was driven out to starve and all of his property went to the state. Now it is a museum.”

Adrian shrugged, “Let’s go.”

The first thing we saw upon entering the gates was a solemn cat staring at us from where it sat at the side of the path.

Another napped in the shade of a bush, and one drowsing on a bench in the sun suffered me to pet it. Within, there was room after room of intricately decorated ceilings and elaborately tiled floors, enormous fireplaces, and patterned window sills. With the way the light slanted in, from openings in the ceiling and narrow, high-set stained glass windows, every room seemed to hold its breath waiting to be born into a painting. I pulled out my camera and took picture after picture of the way the light came in, curving, shaping, carving the rooms, revealing flutters of color, a line of calligraphy in mosaic, an arc in stone. I could sense how to translate it, a touch of ochre here, complemented by the sienna there. The shadows captured in the deep translucent water of cobalt, or perhaps with just a touch of cerulean blue.

Yet even before it could be fully brought to life in my mind I felt defeated, conquered by my own lack of knowledge. I did not know even enough Arabic to speak to the guard at the gate, to ask permission. I felt so restrained by my own inability to communicate, not only in terms of language but with respect to customs. Language seemed so essential. Communication in any country was so enmeshed with culture, history, and the very rhythms of speech seemed tied into the body's gestures. I could remember how after my Spanish classes in Guanajuato it was as though an entire world of perception and understanding had opened up to me. A switch had flipped in my mind and my eyes had truly seen Mexico for the first time.

When it was time to leave I put away my camera and understood that if there was a defeat to be suffered in Morocco, it would be brought on by me. I could only be conquered by my own fear. There were no true distractions, there were only excuses. It wasn't the presence of Adrian or the difficulty of language. It was only me in the end, afraid of failure and afraid to try.

We continued on to the remains of the royal palace, Palais el Badi. Palais el Badi translated to, “the incomparable” and was once reputed to be one of the most beautiful palaces in the world. As we bought our tickets and walked through the gate, I could see all that was left were towering pise walls topped by stork nests. It took Sultan Moulay Ismail ten years to strip the palace of everything moveable or of value. What remained was the ceremonial part of the palace complex created for the reception of ambassadors.

The construction of the palace began shortly after Ahmed el Mansour’s accession. Its finance came from a large ransom paid out by the Portuguese after the Battle of the Three Kings, fought in 1578. Ahmed was dubbed El Mansour (the victorious) and ascended the throne, reigning for twenty-five years. He also seized the gold route across the Sahara and captured Timbuktu which earned him another nickname, El Eddahbi (the Golden).

Before us stretched the central court of the Palace, it was over 430 feet long and almost as wide. The court was originally constructed on a series of vaults in order to allow circulation of water through the pools and sunken gardens. On either side of the pools were summer pavilions, the most prominent being a large hall called the Koubba el Hamsiniya (the fifty pavilions) for the number of its columns. South of the courtyard were the ruins of the palace stables and beyond them a series of dungeons used into the present century as a state prison. It was said that El Mansour rewarded his workers generously, even entertaining their children so his workers would not have any distractions. In contrast, Moulay Ismail who ruled after El Mansour and took apart the Palais el Badi, was known for beating up, starving and entombing his workers where they fell, into the walls of his palaces. On the state opening of the Palais el Badi it was said that Ahmed el Mansour asked his court jester for his opinion of the completed palace and the jester responded that it one day would make a “magnificent ruin.”

I narrowed my gaze until it fell into a soft blur, lines and contours vanishing, light merging into shadow, color bleeding across forms, and tried to imagine the walls, ceilings, and fountains whole. Rich hangings would have covered the naked stones and thick rugs would have lain underfoot to soften the step. The flicker of a startled bird taking flight, the branch of a bush set into motion by a breeze became the movements of the women of the harem, laying carelessly about, awaiting the sultan’s call. With a blink however, the pools became no more than tiled holes naked of water, the gardens sunken pits of straggling greenery, and the columns of the Koubba el Hamsinya broken monoliths of rock.

The roof terrace had a panoramic view of the surrounding medina and just as we climbed to the top the calls to prayer simultaneously droned out from all of the minaret towers. Each tower had a different man conducting the prayer and their words intertwined and separated, coalesced into knots then unraveled into a cacophony of competing voices that rose high above the city. The loudspeakers made the voices nearly mechanical, alien, insect-like. As the cries echoed off the fortified walls, the late afternoon light streaked under low clouds and lit up the line of the city, edging up minaret towers silhouetted against the grey sky. I leaned forward against the stone wall, feeling the rough edges cut into the flesh of my hands and as I did I caught a whiff of sandalwood and spices carried up to me from a hidden shop far below.

“In Baghdad when the prayer rang out it was eerie, the whole city would go silent. All the gunshots would stop and it would get... so damn quiet... The firefights wouldn’t start again until prayer was completed.” I turned to look at Adrian and he stared out at the city as though he was lost. Lost in memories he didn't want to relive, lost in the realization that the call to prayer was not just a part of vacation but once again, would soon be a part of his life. The future lurked hidden behind a sheer veil that was being lifted by degrees and Afghanistan waited, patient as a clever, vicious beast. We stood and watched the lights play through the clouds, listened until the prayer call began to die away. As we turned to make our way back down the stairs he held my hand as tightly as I held his.

We left the palace and made our way through a maze of streets until we found ourselves quite by accident in the Souk el Attarin, the market of the spice vendors. The streets were lined with shops whose storefronts were crowded with different colored powders rising high in conical shapes above metal canisters. We were greeted on all sides by shopkeepers eager to lure us in. I lowered my head and did not allow my steps to falter until I turned to make sure Adrian was behind me and saw he had been ensnared by a spice seller who spoke English. I walked back reluctantly and allowed myself to be pulled inside and sat on a low bench.

"No pressure to buy, only look my friends. Many things here traditional to Morocco, come I will explain them, let me show you. This top shelf here," he pulled down a glass jar from the top shelf filled with pink powder and opened the lid as he spoke "has pigments, for painting. Look, when I add water the color changes." As I watched the soft pink powder became a deep crimson red at the touch of a few drops of liquid. I sat up straight, suddenly paying attention and could feel Adrian shooting me a look. "These small bottles here, they have scented oils for the woman, here Madame, smell. This here..." he pulled down a jar filled with what looked like varying sizes of bars of crumbling soap. He reached in and pulled a small piece out, "this is natural perfume, you rub against the skin, here," he pointed to my wrist. He continued pulling out traditional cosmetics, earthenware saucers of cochineal for rouge, powdered kohl or antimony for darkening the edges of the eyes, sticks of suak (walnut root or bark) which Moroccans used to clean their teeth. He even had grooved circles of clay to pumice dry heels. One white powder he added rose water to and put on my face, demonstrating after ten minutes when it was dry it could be removed with water to leave the skin soft and smooth. He had small tubs of natural oil based soap and I set aside some plain olive oil soap for cleaning my paint brushes. He explained the different kinds of cooking spices he had and let us sniff each one. When we walked out of the store I found Adrian's hands to be empty and in mine I carried a large bag stuffed with purchases, but I could not find it within me to feel regret.

We continued on, stopping now and then but mostly we both felt a little tired of Marrakesh with her constant crush of people, scooters, bikes, cars, and donkeys always pushing us up against buildings, the increasingly cranky and abusive hawkers and the high prices. We ate our dinner in the central square rewarding the most respectful and least pushy waiter by choosing his establishment which served the same food for the same prices as the fifteen other tightly, clustered food stalls. Though we sat on a naked wood bench, under a swaying line of light bulbs, the night sky above us, the market howling around us, our waiter was quick to serve us and the food hot and delicately seasoned. The owner was also the cook and he labored over a grill on a well-lit platform, nearly spotlighted as he worked with an economy of movement in a street performance of his own.

In the square some street entertainers were belly dancing, homage to the god of money and the law of coin as they charged each tourist foolish enough to try to sneak a picture. They were dressed head to toe in white bulky concealing robes and black wrapped cloth hid all of the face but for the eyes. It was a costume that could have hidden the identity of a man as easily as that of a woman. The absence of bare flesh however, was made up for in the flash of kohl rimmed eyes and hips emphasized by a tightly wrapped shawl sewn with glittering clinking coins which thrust and shivered to the beat of the drum. Above us the stars watched, as they did every night, wherever we chose to be, whether it was in the desolate embrace of the Sahara or in the heart of Marrakesh.

A Bengal Tiger Loose on Halloween

10/00

Education is so much more than school. I think of how many years it has taken me to realize this, all the tests I used to study for, only to instantly forget what I had memorized after the exam was over. All of the things I was taught that were supposedly so important and now there are no grades, no roll call is taken. Each one of the students at the Florence Academy comes to class because they are passionate about art, because they fought to be here, to experience this. Every lesson is important, every minute is precious. It's like I am living in a dream. Sometimes I can't believe any of this is real.

On Sunday I went to an exhibition that was showing seventy master drawings. I saw two charcoal sketches by Degas and a sketch for "Leda and the Swan" by Leonardo Da Vinci. Seeing their sketches made them seem more human to me because some of them were not very good. They were probably just scribbling down ideas, little knowing those drawings would be representative of their work and future generations would be lining up and paying to see them. In retrospect I can understand why Michelangelo burned so many of his early sketches.

I spent the rest of the day painting a watercolor study of the view across from my bedroom window: the dome of the Duomo rising into a cloudy sky and below to the right the columns of the biblioteca. I have started an oil painting that will have a still life in the foreground made up of my black fringed shawl, some Italian coins, photographs of local landscapes, and a small bronze statue of a nude woman pulling her hair up off of her neck. I found the bronze statue at a flea market by Lake Cuomo. Behind the still life is my bedroom window with the view and by incorporating the Italian objects with the scenery I hope to have a unified Italian theme. I figure maybe I will stay sane doing these unending Bargue drawings at school if I can work on my own painting projects in my free time.

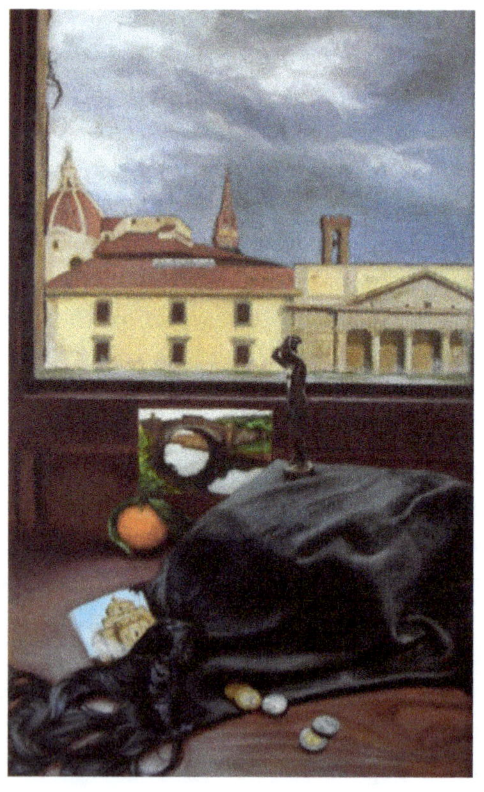

My roommates and I threw a Halloween party the other evening. It was my Swedish roommate, Linda's idea and we hung black paper bats from the ceiling and black paper spiders in the kitchen. We made a bunch of food and told

everyone to bring something to eat or drink. Linda even drew up invitations with a little map on it, complete with a drawing of the Arno River with a black Arno rat swimming across.

I got a picture of an albino Bengal tiger out of a magazine and using that and some old paint brushes painted my face white with black stripes in the tiger's facial pattern, then had fake fang teeth which slipped over my incisors. Linda dressed as a vampire geisha and painted her face white with a pink spot on each cheek; she had bright red bow lips and vampire teeth.

Our main circle of friends was the first to show up and then somehow the party caught on. I remember seeing one of the more popular students shouting into his cell phone, while standing in our hallway, that it was a 'raging party, to drop everything and come over.' Around 2 am there was a limbo contest in my living room using a broom. I stayed pretty sober because I was sure any moment the carabinieri were going to show up, banging on my door and demanding to speak to the tenant responsible for the noise. I figured someone being able to speak Italian had to appear properly in charge. Yet, there were no noise complaints and no carabinieri. It made me feel very expansive towards our upstairs neighbors after that, even when they threw parties on their verandah which doubles as the ceiling of my bedroom.

The party kept growing, at least three quarters of the school showed up and that included faculty. At 3 am one of the sculpture instructors was crawling around on her hands and knees upending empty wine bottles and howling, "We need more alcohol!" We let her crash on our couch, which was around the time people began to leave.

I started cleaning up and in the dining room, Linda freaked out when she saw what looked like a large pile of poop in the shadowy corner behind a chair. We were both horrified, thinking, 'My god, these people are animals.' I was the least squeamish and on closer inspection realized that it was a large slice of chocolate fudge cake that had fallen on the red tile floor. We had a good laugh over that. There was a lot of trash. One girl had come as a mermaid, she had made a large attachable paper and wire tail that she ended up discarding halfway through the night because it was too big and kept getting in the way. I grumbled loudly that the least she could have done, was to take it with her. The next morning the passed out sculpture instructor was late to school.

On Friday one of the students came up to me in class and asked what was on for the night. I was surprised he would ask me but said, "Um, well, we could go play pool at this pool hall I know about." The word apparently got passed around because by evening half the school showed up to play pool at my pool hall. It was a local hangout filled with mainly Italian guys who stop playing and gawk when a female dares to enter their sanctum. I think everyone was tired of meeting at the pub every Friday night and sitting around, shouting to be heard over the music. So comparatively, this was quite successful and not greatly expensive either, especially if you have three to four people to a table. I am not much of a pool player but I am slowly learning.

The heat was finally turned on in our apartment. It isn't fancy; you can't turn it off or down. It is either on when it wants to be, or its not on if it doesn't feel like it. Some of the other students either have no heat at all, heat for one hour of the day, or heat they can turn on that works badly and they have to pay an extra 70,000 lira a month for. Mine, of course, is included in the rent and is quite satisfying. In fact sometimes it gets so warm in our apartment, no small feat considering the 20 foot high ceilings, that we throw open the huge windows to cool it down.

It has been raining buckets lately, my poor hiking boots are worn out and my feet get soaked within minutes. I have been drawing all day at school with wet feet; many fellow sufferers have been home sick resulting from the same thing. Yesterday I went to the open market of San Ambrogio, picked through bins of slightly used boots and found a pair of leather combat boots with thick rubber soles that fit quite well. At the same market I bought a pair of cheap gloves and cut the fingers off. They will be my drawing gloves because the school is not well heated. Some second year students told me to wear a hat, gloves, scarf, and cut a piece of cardboard to put under my work area because otherwise the cold of the floor seeps up through your shoes into your feet.

This week I have been going to school early at 7:30am instead of 9:00am and staying till 7pm and Saturday I came in at 10am and stayed till 7:30pm and I have to go in again Sunday. I am determined to be ahead, two other students have started work on their cast drawings before me. After this project I am working on however, I will be allowed to move on to cast work as well.

* * *

It has been a long day, we had figure drawing in the evening which is pretty intense and it separates the determined die hard artists from the wimpy ones. After eight hours of drawing and squinting at your project, your legs hurt, your hands are numb from the cold, your eyes sore, brain befuddled, and stomach screaming for supper but at 5 pm sharp the model steps up and you find out which among you has reserves and which among you is a whiner at heart. I did pretty well but by 7pm I was definitely crawling home and hungry enough I was no longer interested in food.

There is a plump, amiable, black and white cat who likes to come into the school and loudly purring, demand attention. He is known for wandering into the figurative drawing class, meowing an inquiry at the model, then rubbing against the modeling platform. He is always dumped unceremoniously outside before he is tempted to rub against the model's bare ankle, but always returns less than five minutes later, insistent on affection.

The other day we were drawing the model when from overhead there was snarl, followed by a deafening screech. We couldn't figure out where it was coming from, it sounded like a cat being stepped on or squashed. The screaming continued, very distracting and we realized looking up through the skylights that it was two cats on the roof fighting. Finally the screaming stopped and it was just one cat doing that warning, snarling, moaning sound they make. It definitely put everyone's neck hair on end. It continued for ten minutes, loud enough to reverberate through the school. Then there was a climactic screech followed by a thumping, tumbling, pounding, before it went quiet. It sounded like they fell right off the edge of the roof. I think it was our puss declaring that this was his flipping school and no other cat was welcome. Haven't seen him for days though, I hope he won.

* * *

Today is my sheet washing day, I have a clothes line permanently strung up between the headboard of my bed and the top hinge of the bathroom door. When I hang my sheets there to dry, since we have a washing machine but no dryer, it is impossible to get anything else done because I am always ducking around them and still getting wacked in the face. It is Saturday however and I plan to go into school today for sculpture class.

The night before we had a dinner party and served Thai food, then went to a movie playing in an old restored theater, it has a brass railed balcony section and huge red velvet curtains which hang in every entryway that you have to fight your way through. Afterwards three of us girls rode a beautiful hand carved carousel in front of the Palazzo Strozzi. The horses had real horse hair tails and manes, mirrors inlaid on their haunches, bodies brightly painted and the dangling reins had lace sewn onto them. The music was playing a delirious tune and on top of my horse, with the air fresh from the rain brushing my face, surrounded by the old buildings of Florence, I thought to myself, 'I am really here, I made it.'

Chapter 4

Taroudannt: From Guide to Model

"I asked Bob what was the key to living such a great story... and he said he didn't think we should be afraid to embrace whimsy. I asked him what he meant by whimsy and he struggled to define it. He said it's that nagging idea that life could be magical; and it could be special if we were only willing to take a few risks."
–Donald Miller A Million Miles in a 1000 Years

9/12/07

I took another sip of coffee as I checked the cheap, plastic, replacement watch I had recently purchased from a street vendor, then shifted nervously in my seat.. The silence was broken only by the soft gurgle of the fountain that with each splash seemed to be counting down minutes, seconds, lost and never to be regained.

Adrian looked up from his breakfast at me, "You'll be fine. You will probably enjoy being alone again for a little while and besides I will meet up with you again in about a week. I wish you were coming with me." He was flying south to Guinea, a country on the west coast of Africa to see his sister who worked for the American ambassador there. It had been an expensive plane ticket however, and a complicated tourist visa to obtain so I had decided to remain in Morocco and continue traveling on my own.

I swallowed and stared down into my cup, I wanted to reach across the space and touch him again. I wanted to say something, anything which wasn't goodbye. I could feel fear and uncertainty climbing up my spine with cool pinprick fingers and to shake it off and push it back I checked my watch again, "I've got to go." I stood and shrugged on my pack and Adrian followed me as I walked toward the door. I took one quick look back as I reached the street to where he stood in the lobby motionless, silent, watching me.

I hailed a taxi and arrived at the bus station to an artful confusion of milling people, long lines, and incomprehensible signs. I stood with the ticket I had purchased the day before clutched in my sweating hand and was reminded of all the different bus stations I had gone through in Mexico, and the time it had taken for me to grow comfortable with traveling by myself in a foreign country. As I stood there I felt lost, my shield, my translator, my security was gone. I had to make decisions for myself now, I had to take charge.

I caught a hint of English in my vicinity and was able to pick out a smattering of white skin, fellow tourists. Without shame I eavesdropped on their conversation and found out that I needed to check my bags before boarding, at the ticket desk. The bus turned out to be huge and comfortable with assigned seats, cool air, and a bus driver who was an artist at passing cars on single lane twisting roads. As I watched him from my seat perched immediately up and behind him, I realized several things, the first was that his speedometer was broken and the second was that there was an elaborate spoken language involving the horn. It was used to tell bicyclists to edge off the road, to tell the vehicle in front of us we were passing, to acknowledge the person who had honked to say he was passing you, and it was used if the person in front of you was barely going ten miles an hour and you had to slam on your brakes to keep from hitting him.

The bus let me off in Inezgane, a town where, according to the bus ticket agent in Marrakesh, I could catch a taxi to Taroudannt, my final destination. As I stood next to my bus I saw at least three different types of taxis pass at full speed up and down the road directly before me and it was not immediately apparent where I needed go. I retraced my steps to ask and the bus driver pointed me across the street. On the other side I found a lot full of parked vacant taxis and when I spoke to the nearest lounging taxi driver I was told it would cost me 250 dirham to get to Taroudannt. I eyed him with suspicion because the ticket agent had said it should cost me less than 100 dirham. When I mentioned this, the taxi driver and his cronies informed me in broken English that this was not the case and alone I could expect no less of a price. At which point one of them muttered something about the colectiv taxi which reminded me of information I had read in my book.

A colectiv taxi was cheaper because you shared it with other people going the same direction, whereas a privately hired taxi was much more expensive. When I asked about the colectiv I was told I would not be interested in it, at which point I walked away. Every potential taxi driver I saw after that I asked, "Colectiv? Taroudannt?" and I was continuously pointed ever onwards. At last, after asking two men standing by an idling taxi the same question, they exchanged glances, gave a few snorts of amusement at my expense and then stuffed me into the front bucket seat of a small taxi practically on top of an already sitting well rounded, shrouded Arab woman with, I noticed on the drive, surprisingly hairy legs. We smiled at each other as two complete strangers welded together at the hip often do smile. The backseat was stuffed with three others also headed to Taroudannt and for a mere fifteen dirham we were off.

According to my book the Saadians made Taroudannt their capital in the 16th century and built most of its circuit of walls. Taroudannt had 5km of ramparts that surrounded it, they were the best preserved medina walls in Morocco, and their color changed from golden brown to deep red depending on the time of day. At first glance when we drove into the center, the town didn't seem like much, the medina was surrounded by crenellated brown walls, inside of which the buildings seemed identical, all painted a matching brown with occasional stained glass windows.

After I checked into my hotel I decided to go out and explore. My goal, now that I was alone, was to find painting subjects and begin to paint. It was difficult to pinpoint exactly what I was looking for however, I needed a subject that was not just visually inspiring but also located in an environment conducive to painting for up to seven hours. As I stopped to consider a sun dappled alleyway I found myself calculating whether the effect in the alley was only a result of the fall of the light and if it was, how long I would have before the light began to change. Was I going to be disturbed continuously by curious passerby? Was I going to be in the way of traffic? I had only my experiences in Mexico to refer to for painting outside of the studio. I mentally reviewed the subjects I had found to paint there even as I walked through the streets hoping to be inspired by something, anything.

Taroudannt was considered far enough off the tourist beaten track that my guidebook while recommending it, had not furnished a city map and I quickly got lost. I stumbled onto the compulsory market after a series of zigzagging lefts and rights I had made in the hopes of finding a familiar street. The bazaar seemed no different than any of the other ones I had yet been to, except somewhat smaller. It was still busy and chaotic enough that I knew trying to paint it would be difficult. For an entry project, I needed something simple, set in a peaceful secluded spot. As I walked, the sight I found the most fascinating were the shrouded women who made their way down the street in pairs. Though their robes covered them completely they still seemed to express sensuality through color. The scarves bound tightly over their heads to hide their hair only seemed to accentuate the jewel of the revealed face and when the nose down was covered with a black scarf it brought all the more attention to the swift nightingale flicker of the eyes, the brows creating dark exotic pools of shadow. I realized I didn't want to spend my trip painting the same interiors, landscapes, and ruins that I had focused on in Mexico. I wanted to take the next step. I wanted to work with people again. Yet, to approach one of those women seemed next to impossible, even if I could speak the same language.

With Adrian gone, I realized I was no longer invisible. In my stained dusty pants, sagging black shirt, wisps of hair sticking out from my braid I passed endless numbers of men lingering or sitting off the street and their combined stares were as intimidating as the warning growl issued from a pack of dogs. I could not recall ever being the focus of attention as a girl in Italy or even last year in Mexico and I felt myself begin to walk faster. The only other unveiled women on the street in pants were foreigners and I saw precious few of them. As I walked I met no one's eye and though I was lightheaded with hunger every restaurant/café was packed with men watching people pass and I was afraid to stop and even look at a menu.

Finally in desperation I paused in the main square near my hotel and stood nervously on the sidewalk eyeing a displayed menu for all of seconds before a waiter approached and looked me up and down in silence. He made a tentative sweep of his arm towards his restaurant and I gave a nod of agreement. He ushered me past table after table of staring men until we were inside where there were yet more men sitting watching sports on TV. At my look of dismay he pointed up at the second floor and as I nodded, he looked relieved as he led the way. The top floor was empty of people and I sat at a window with a view of the square. He shook his head to each item on the menu that I pointed at and I realized they were out of many of their menu options. I wished that I could simply ask him for a plate of food, 'un plato de comida,' like what was advertised in the loncherias of Mexico. Finally when I pointed at noodles in red sauce, he nodded, gave a small bow and left. I realized then, we had conversed perfectly without ever exchanging a word and I could not help but feel amused that I was in the same position I had been in when I had first arrived in Mexico a year ago: struggling to find somewhere to eat.

* * *

"Good morning, Madame."

I looked up nervously at the man who stood in front of my table as I sipped my second cup of coffee, "Good morning."

"You have recently arrived? I am a local guide. Maybe you are interested in tour of Taroudannt?"

I considered for a moment. Yesterday's explorations had not turned up any painting subjects and I was a little worried. The hotel itself was visually interesting. It had originally been a French Foreign Legion building and in its present incarnation as a two-story hotel exhibited glowing pink painted walls, turquoise tile work, and a central courtyard with a large fake giraffe, and saddled wooden horse posed next to a group of palm trees. I could find a painting composition here easily and yet nothing moved me. I nodded slowly, "How much?" He named a not unreasonable price and after brief negotiations we agreed that after breakfast he would give me a three hour walking tour of the city.

I finished my coffee and rejoined him in the lobby. The tour took me to the top of the ramparts of the Kasbah where a man was carving sculptures out of limestone, then down through a series of blacksmith stalls. I was left at a rug shop called Ali Baba which I dove out of frantically, then I was taken to a silversmith to watch him make jewelry. In the heart of a market we stopped at an open yard filled with large piles of grain where robed women sat on the dirt with sifters that they used to sort out impurities before the grain was bagged for buyers. While we walked he taught me some Arabic words and told me a little about the town, how it was populated by three quarters Berber people and only a quarter Arabs and that the town was conservative and very traditional.

While we were walking we came across a man standing in rags who held his hands out and murmured in supplication. I watched as my guide stopped to give him some change.

"When I was traveling in Mexico I was scolded for giving money to a beggar. I was told that I should spend my money on people who work for a living and not encourage lazy people to beg," I said as we continued on.

He shrugged, "Yes, but it is okay to give a little money, a very little. A few coins, it is not so much."

"And what can explain the steep path to you?
It is the freeing of a slave,
Or the giving of food in a day of starvation."-Koran

Next, I was taken to a shop where they ground down seeds to make argon oil which they used in women's cosmetics. The Argan tree was unique to Morocco and similar to the olive tree.

It grew on the lower slopes of mountains and goats were known to climb up the trunks and stand on the branches in order to eat the leaves, a sight I had seen when driving through the outskirts of the Atlas Mountains on the group tour. I bought a tube of green lipstick made from Argon oil that turned a bright lush red when it came into contact with the skin.

I checked my watch as we left the shop, the tour was nearly over and I was in exactly the same quandary as I was in before we had started. I had seen many things that held potential, the blacksmiths crouched over a shower of sparks, the shrouded women sorting grains in the market, the sculptor chiseling limestone atop the walls but realistically I ran into the same problem as before, I couldn't speak the language. How was I to communicate? How was I to hire someone? I considered my guide as he walked next to me and tried to choose my words carefully. "Maybe you can help me with something. I will be in Taroudannt for a few days and I am looking to hire someone for a very easy job. I am a painter and I need someone to sit still for me so I can paint them." He gave me a confused look. "Painter... artist..." I pantomimed holding a brush to canvas.

He nodded slowly, "This is possible, what sort of person do you want?"

I took a breath and tried to quell the hope that suddenly ignited in my chest, "Anyone, anyone at all, only they must not dress western, only traditional clothes, man, woman, anyone. Maybe you have a friend who wants an easy job? I will pay."

"When would you need this person?"

"Today, this afternoon, tomorrow, every day, whenever they are free." He nodded and appeared deep in thought. We walked a block in silence as I held my breath.

"Perhaps me, Madame? I am free this afternoon, how much do you pay?"

I looked at him carefully but tried not to seem as though I was studying him. He was a middle- aged man with a moustache, there was little to make him seem terribly remarkable, he was neither tall nor short, neither fat nor thin, he was not beautiful but then he was not ugly. It was difficult to tell actually, because he wore a plain button up shirt and pants, his head was bare, he looked like a man who could be from anywhere. "You have traditional clothes?"

"Of course Madame, of course, also a friend of mine has a shop. You want perhaps the Berber djellaba and the head covering?"

"Yes, that would be perfect. I could pay you the same for three hours as I paid you now for this tour. It is easier money to earn. You have been walking for three hours in the heat, to model for me you only have to sit. It is very simple. You could pose for me today in the courtyard of my hotel, at 1pm maybe?"

He dropped me off at my hotel, agreeing to meet in a couple hours and I raced about securing a sandwich and fries for a dollar at a takeaway place across the way. I noticed the piercing stares of the local men were back. As my guide had accompanied me through the streets I had gained a cloak of invisibility but apparently it had been temporary. They were quiet at least. In Italy the men were noisy about their observations; here if a man did speak it was only to murmur, "Bon jour" as I passed.

After securing food I dashed back to my room to organize art supplies and prep my paints. I tried to remember if I had been as nervous and unsure when beginning my first painting in Mexico. It had been a long time since I had last tried to paint a portrait and I could not help but doubt myself. I busied myself in the steps I knew by heart, making piles of paint with my palette knife, arranging my turpentine and mineral spirits, taping a sheet of canvas to my foam-core travel board. I let my doubts build and did not struggle against them. I let them accelerate my breath, make my heart pound, my hands tremble and then I let them wash over and through me, past me. I had found talent and ability in art counted for little, what was more important, and harder to find was the courage to try and continue trying even if the result was not always successful. The driving passion that found inspiration in a trick of light, a subtle movement, a delicate gesture had to be stronger than doubt and fear. I had to want to paint for the love of creation, the peace found in observation; not out of a desire for any societal definition of success.

He was, perhaps, a little unsure as well because he showed up in regular clothes to make sure I was there, and then disappeared. He was back minutes later in a long blue robe, the djellaba, worked with gold embroidery and a blue and black head wrap. He settled into the chair I had set out for him under a white archway with a deep, cobalt blue, paned window in the background and surrounding aqua colored tiles. The djellaba was like a gown, and yet managed to be utterly masculine. It writhed around his form with a life of its own and the gold embroidery served as punctuating calligraphy, tracing out folds and catching the light in subdued sparks. With the head wrap his face looked darker. The blue brought out the deep ambers, greens, and reds of his skin and the shadows surrounding his eyes made his gaze seem distant and remote. He was transformed, a different man. My gap toothed guide had vanished and been replaced by someone elusive, intangible.

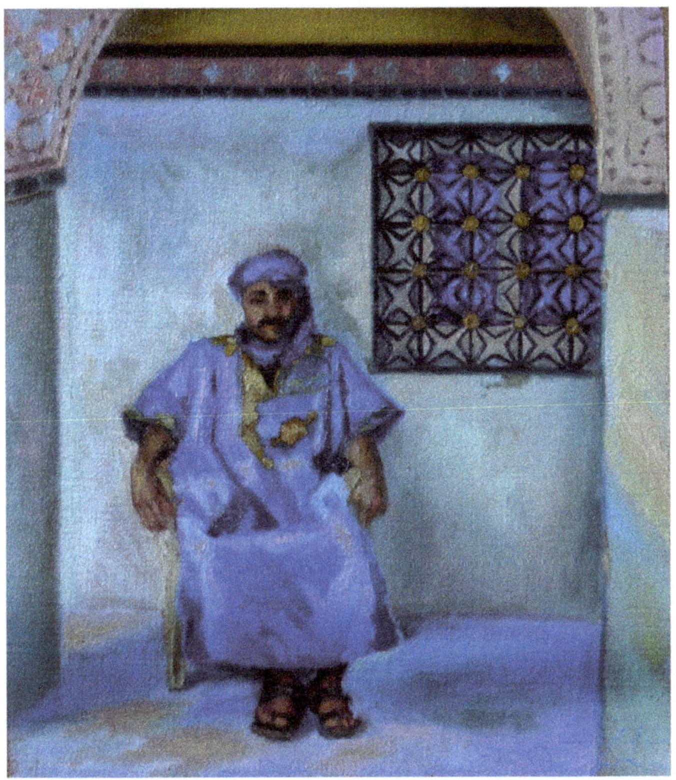

It was a difficult composition, there were so many shades of blue, yet the tones were different and the way the indirect light shaped the space was subtle. He sat in a chair staring straight ahead and yet conveying that sense of him sitting, sinking back and down, at rest, yet watchful, with that hint of waiting, seemed just beyond my reach. When I mixed my paints I tried to focus only on the sense of light, the large patterns, ignoring the subject matter and searching for rhythms. I had thought at first to work on only his portrait from the shoulders up but I was ambitious. I could not bring myself to cut out his surroundings.

At the end of the day I was sweaty and tired, losing track of time so the poor man sat half an hour longer than was necessary.

As he stood and stretched, I backed up from my sketch and was disappointed. It had been too complex a project for my first painting, too much to fit on such a small space. He had done an excellent job, keeping his breaks short and always striving to find the correct pose, holding as still as he was able. The space, as well, was perfect, a few hotel guests had passed through the courtyard but had been polite and left me to work.

I knew the main problem lay in my own nervousness, my hesitance, my impatience which pushed me into detail too quickly. My sketch held all the main points of the model but lacked any sense of atmosphere or subtlety. It was a barely recognizable rendering of my subject and while I could work on it again the following day, I decided to change my approach. I resolved to begin a new painting the next morning, a simple portrait, and in spite of the long tedious sitting he agreed to return.

* * *

He arrived right on time at ten the following morning. Unlike the day before, I had given myself enough time to get thoroughly prepared by the time he came: my paints were mixed, my work area situated, caffeine was surging through my veins and my thoughts were focused. I had him stay in his costume but move closer to me and I disregarded the background. I kept the entire gesture loose and right away the new painting was more solid. I found myself relaxing instead of reliving the struggle of the day before. I thought about the elaborate tile work behind him and the precision and attention to detail in the adornment of the medersas in Fes. It all seemed to underline how important it was to enjoy the process of creating, rather than focus merely on the end result.

It was easy to see the difference when a finished piece was rushed or forced out. There was less of a flow, a serenity in the execution. My instructor Kamille used to emphasize to me how important it was that a painting appeared to be effortless when it was completed rather than struggled over and worked. The strongest paintings looked nearly accidental, almost careless even if they were meticulously planned. John Singer Sargent could lay in the plane of an upper lip in a single brush stroke but there were times when that came after he had scrapped an entire painting or scraped out the upper lip each time he had laid it in wrong. Most likely there were times he had to paint in that brush stroke over and over until with a single lay in, it was suddenly perfect, exactly how he had planned it, exactly how he had envisioned it in his mind. But he could not be impatient, he could not rush the execution, it had to come on its own, it had to be found, discovered, learned.

The sympathetic accent of my model's brow, the laugh lines at the edges of his eyes, the mouth that curved a little at the corners of his moustache hinting at a face constantly creased by smiles, all suggested his character. I felt that to attempt to reproduce his features was to try to understand the man, to wonder at his life and story.

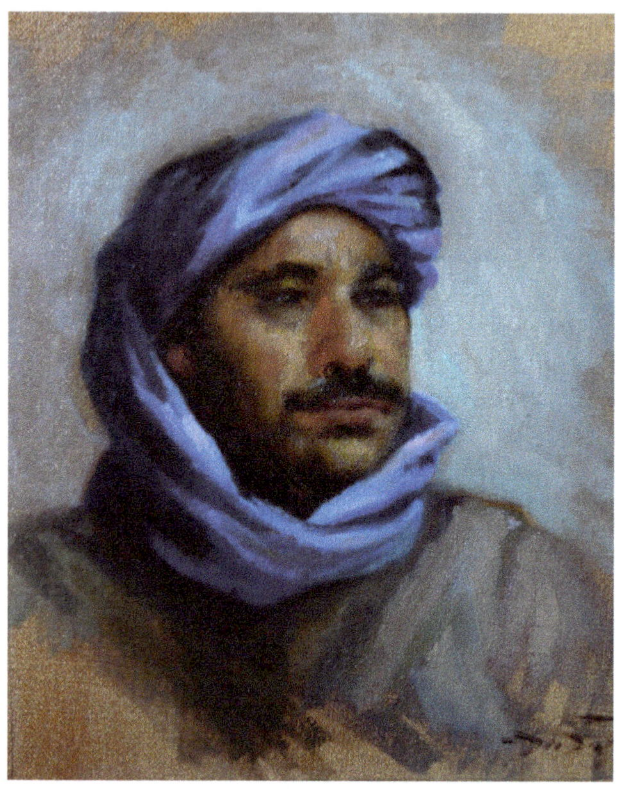

On his break he came and stood behind me to check on my progress, the day before he could not wait for the painting to form. "Where are my arms?" he would ask. "Are you going to paint the gold in the djellaba? You should paint the bars on the window."

With the portrait he watched it come together with amusement and when it was done I asked him if he liked it, if he thought it looked like him. "Yes!" he said laughing, "it is me, exactly."

"Perhaps," I said frowning, "but I think my picture is too serious, you are always smiling."

"No, look," he said pointing at the portrait's moustache, "you can see the smile a little there." He was very proud; while he was posing he asked each passerby to come and look at what I was doing and tell him if it was good.

While we were working on the portrait the owner of the hotel entered and my model immediately leapt up bowing. "Madame," he whispered. "This man is the head boss of the hotel. Very important man." I was unsure if I should take my paint palette off of my lap and stand or if it was okay to continue to sit. I decided I was a tourist and offered my hand, telling my interpreter to communicate how beautiful I thought the hotel was. It was translated back to me that the boss liked my painting and wondered if I would paint a large picture of the interior of his hotel for him, he would pay me. I explained that I did not have a large canvas with me, only small ones and I would only be there a day or so more because I had to meet someone in Essaouira.

We exchanged a few more pleasantries before he left murmuring, "Insh' allah." Which I was told meant," As God wills it." My model, I could tell, was disappointed. I couldn't help but feel selfishly possessive of my time however, and the need to keep art the one thing in my life uncomplicated by other people's demands and expectations.

When I emerged from the hotel to look for lunch I was greeted by thick honey flavored, sun coated silence, a ghost town peopled by not even a stray breeze. Everywhere I looked doors and windows were barred and suddenly I remembered offering to buy my model a soda only an hour before, from the hotel bar and how he had gently shook his head. The holy month of Ramadan had begun and Muslims were not allowed to eat or drink from sunrise to sunset each day for the entire month. Because the Muslim calendar was based on the cycle of the moon which was twenty-eight days, the month of Ramadan began and ended with the sighting of the new moon and took place in different seasons from year to year. It celebrated the time when the sayings of Muhammad were gathered together in the Koran.

Some of the religious duties of a Muslim were to observe the requirements of Ramadan, give money to the poor, make a hadji (a pilgrimage to Mecca) and show faith by praying five times a day at dawn, noon, afternoon, sunset, and when night fell. Muezzins were issued from the top of the mosque minaret towers and called the faithful to prayer; a Muslim could pray anywhere but had to face the city of Mecca while praying. The end of Ramadan was celebrated with a huge festival and feast called Aid el- Fitr, which I would unfortunately miss since I would be leaving Morocco less than a week before Ramadan would end.

As I surveyed the closed shuttered street I realized I had not really had any concept of what Ramadan meant or how it would impact my trip. In front of a small shop a woman stood on the pavement grilling plain unseasoned Moroccan crepes and I was grateful and relieved as I bought one and a bottle of water to take back to my hotel.

That afternoon I was trying to resolve the background of my painting from the day before in an attempt to study and push the effect when my model stuck his head around the corner. "Hello Madame. I have just come to check, you will wait in the hotel courtyard tonight and I will come to tell you whether I can return tomorrow."

I nodded, "Yes, I will be here."

"Maybe I will be here around 7:30; we can get some dinner together."

I eyed him warily and was unsure how to take his suggestion. I could not help but wonder if perhaps it was more than a friendly offer and he had come to the wrong conclusion as a result of my spending so much time with him. Had I been too friendly? Had he misinterpreted my single-minded focus? "Thank you but dinner is not necessary, just come by and let me know if you can make it tomorrow. If you can't, bring me a friend, maybe a family member, someone who needs work."

He smiled a little nervously, "Yes Madame, I will come by tonight." He nodded and hovered in the doorway looking uncertain, before turning and leaving. With a sigh I conceded to myself that while we might be speaking the same verbal language, there was a wealth that could not be communicated or understood because of the large cultural gap between us.

* * *

There was no transition between sleeping and waking, I opened my eyes and could envision my plan for the day. It was only 7am but I gathered my supplies and mapped out a quick charcoal drawing on canvas of the upper hallway which I wanted to paint in the afternoon. My model had come by the night before and promised to return to sit for me at 10. I had just enough time to clean up, eat breakfast and then set up for him.

He arrived right on time but had been unable to bring a red head wrap as I had requested. The ones stocked at his friend's shop were too small to wrap properly so he had brought a brilliant orange, yellow and white scarf. I sat back and watched as he twisted it up deftly then sat in a chair facing me. I had decided to work on another portrait of him, but this one in a different area of the courtyard. In the new spot, the tiles behind him were cream colored as opposed to blue and as a result the light that reflected back onto his face was far warmer. When he settled into his spot he unconsciously leaned his head back, lifted his chin, and tilted his head ever so slightly to one side.

I was surprised as I always was by him; he was one of those rare models who transformed when posing. It was as though he threw off a cloak to display a secret character or perhaps instead, he anticipated the persona I was looking for and created it, like an actor, stretching into a new identity.

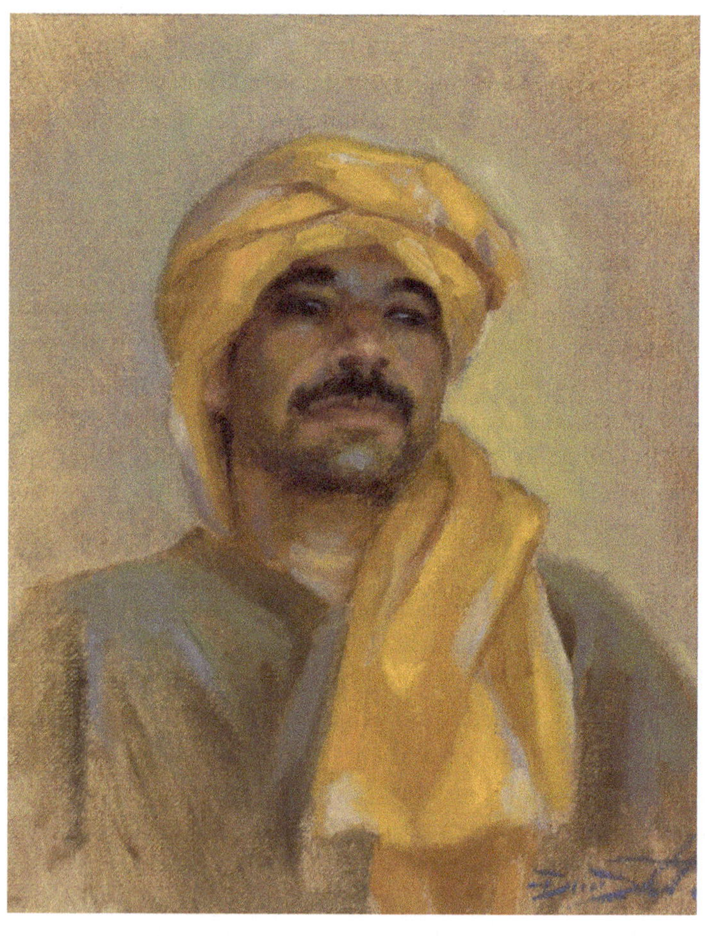

His face and form were so commonplace that I felt sure I would have had difficulty picking him out from a crowd of Moroccan men. When he sat for me however, there was a balance between the symmetry of his features and the expression of his eyes and mouth. There was a certain liquid quality to his gaze, a firmness to his jaw, a strength to the cords of his neck. The yellow scarf I had disliked on sight brought out all of the delicate greens, faint blues, and blushing reds in his skin. It was a complement to his swarthy complexion and gave him an indefinable glow.

In only two hours the painting fell together and I liked the overall effect better than the portrait completed the day before. What I found interesting was that it looked less like my model than the first painting. The second painting, in a trick of light and color, was almost too lovely to be him. The posture was at once languid and proud, the painting technique was more natural and relaxed, yet it wasn't him. Earlier I had looked at the first portrait, after having let it sit all night, and realized there were still quite a few underlying drawing errors: one of the eyes needed to move down, the mouth slightly over and the shadow shape made more unified under the left cheekbone. Yet, there was a very definite likeness I was afraid to lose by tinkering with it too much.

After stretching and stowing my supplies I went out to hunt for lunch and discovered the woman making crepes the day before was nowhere to be found. I walked up and down the closed streets until finally I found a tiny shop open. I settled for a few bananas and a container of yogurt which I took back to my room and combined with an emergency ration granola bar I had brought from the states.

I spent the afternoon on the hotel's upstairs verandah working on the painting of the hallway that I had started in the morning. An outdoor wall, painted a virulent pink, was speckled with sunlight which teased from between overhead tree branches, and it was set with a door framed in patterned tile. The door opened onto a corridor webbed in a lacework of shadow, interrupted only by a series of reflections glittering off the tiled walls and floor like ripples on a pond of water. A blue paned window at the far end let in a cool refraction of indirect light and above hung a row of simple iron candelabra. It had an effect brought on by the afternoon light that was a study in contrasting strong colors and plain architecture.

I was challenged and inspired by the subject but as time wore on my enthusiasm faded as I grew hot and tired. I kept moving my seat back and forth trying to stay in the shade of the tree as the sun shifted. I was assaulted by flies which I tried to ignore then constantly twitched and swatted, like the victim of a nervous tic. Finally I had to admit to myself that my focus was gone and I packed up for the day.

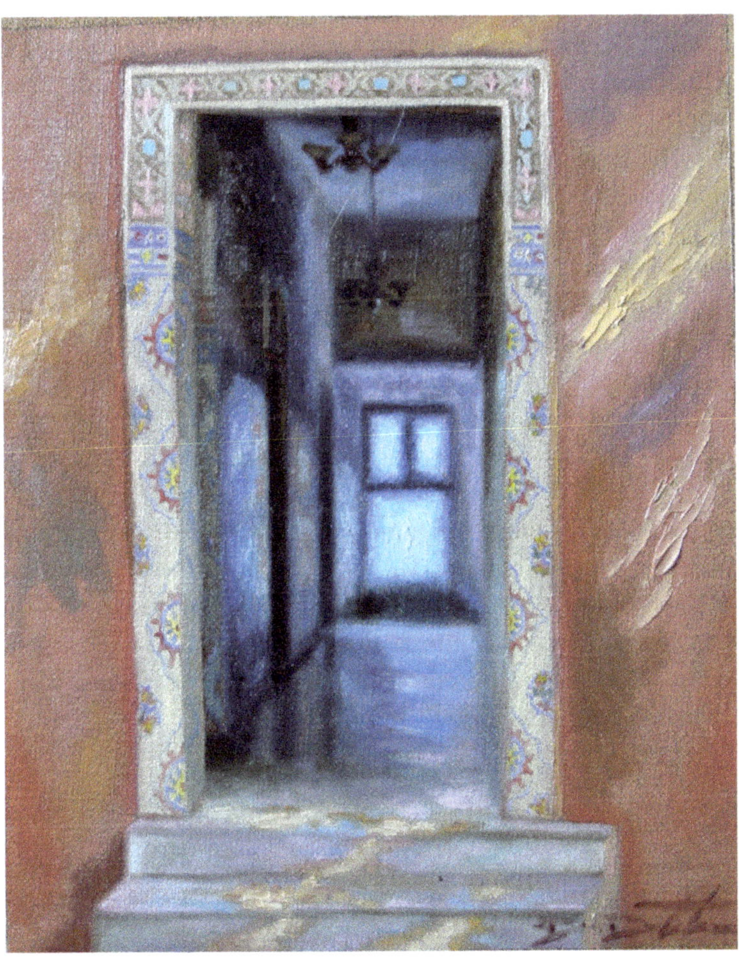

I spent the remainder of the afternoon cleaning my palette, organizing my things, making plans, and getting change. I put all of my paintings out in the sun hoping they would dry in time to be packed the next day. Dinner came in the form of two hot crepes straight from the street grill which I ate right from the bag because they were too hot to touch, accompanied by a cold beer from the hotel's bar. Undernourished cats circled me yowling as I ate and were it not for another guest trying to sit at a table and relax I would have fed them. I knew however, they would turn their sights on him once I left.

The most persistent one was a small black and white cat. Nearly a kitten, he made up for his lack of size in the loudness of his yowls and his ferocity of temperament when one of the other cats got too close or tried to eat what he considered his. He was used to being shooed away because he did not allow me to touch him. Though in the hopes of a handout he sat on my table and as I scuttled my hand closer and closer to him, fingers wiggling, he reached out a paw, almost painfully, as though it were by instinct alone and no great desire on his part, to bat at my fingers. Then, when it seemed he might actually make contact with my hand, he leapt back and assumed an air of great indifference. As he pretended to be fascinated with something in the opposite direction of me, I snuck my hand the rest of the way forward, without him noticing, and tapped on one of his little white paws. He immediately catapulted into the air and vanished under the table.

* * *

I sat up tangled in sheets, it was still dark but I could not sleep anymore. Tired of tossing and turning I got up slowly. My stomach felt strange but I passed it off to nervousness and took a few Pepto Bismol tablets before showering and packing my things. My paintings were nearly dry which made packing easier. I had a specially designed lightweight wood frame that could store up to two wet paintings at once without them coming into contact with each other or anything else.

I lumbered out of my hotel, heaving my bags behind me and skipping breakfast in order to make better time. The man at the front desk flagged down a local taxi for me, put my bags in the trunk and I was dropped off at a collectiv taxi bound for Agadir. This time I was sandwiched in the front seat with a slimmer woman so the ride was not as uncomfortable, though the car exhaust fumes were very strong and made it difficult to breathe.

When I got to Agadir I caught a local taxi to the bus station and as we pulled up I could see a single bus out front idling with a few remaining bags being packed into the luggage compartment. I raced inside and stood in line behind two female tourists who were arguing with the ticket lady and struggling with the language barrier. I tried to curb my impatience without much success, shifting my weight from side to side and looking over my shoulder every few seconds at the waiting bus. Finally they gave up, throwing their hands in the air with a gesture of disgust. They didn't have the right change and the ticket lady could not break their large bill so they left to find a bank. I hurried up to the window and discovered the bus outside was going to Essaouira. This was a piece of luck. I hadn't been able to find out what the bus schedule was and had been afraid I would arrive at the station only to be told the only bus had left earlier or would not leave until evening. I had just enough time to race to a shop and grab a bottle of water and some mango juice before boarding.

As I settled back into my cushioned seat I breathed a sigh of relief. It was a first class bus going directly to Essaouira and I anticipated the rest of the trip to be straightforward and hassle free. We pulled out of town and between one look and the next we had left the flat arid plains behind and were driving along the coast, passing beach after pristine beach, empty for the most part and sprinkled by tiny coastal towns. Above, there wasn't a cloud in the sky. The sun shone down to sparkle off the incoming waves and everything was perfect until suddenly it wasn't. Suddenly there was something very wrong. My vision began to grey out and I could hear a roaring in my ears. Only semi-conscious I threw up all over myself then on the seat next to me which was thankfully empty. When I was done I sat back shivering barely aware of my surroundings, only that the air-conditioning suddenly seemed too strong, nearly subarctic. I sensed the man sitting behind me get up and move but other than that nothing. Silence reigned on the bus. Nobody even turned around. My vision began to clear up and I distracted myself from my soiled clothes by looking out the window at the scenery. Privately I mourned the fact that there was no bathroom on the bus. I had napkins to clean up with but they were safely locked in my bag in the storage compartment down below.

Half an hour later it began again, the tickling numbness, the spots that began to devour my vision but it was worse than before, far worse because I had nothing left to get rid of. I lay face down across the seats heaving helplessly and shivering, lacking even the strength to sit back up in my seat. I knew this time no one would help me, no one would turn around and ask if I was okay, if they should get the driver to stop the bus. At the same time, even as I lay there, I struggled to be quiet. I was afraid of being too ill to finish the bus ride, the driver would put me off in some nameless town and I would be unable to meet up with Adrian the next day like I had promised. I listened to the sound of my heartbeat and concentrated on my breathing until finally I found the strength to sit back up in my seat. I curled my arms around myself and huddled, trying to build an illusion of warmth. I had never felt so alone. About forty-five minutes later the lady in front of me began to throw up but her husband provided a plastic bag and napkins so there was no mess.

An hour later the driver stopped the bus for a bathroom break, though he was the only one to get off the bus. I was afraid of trying to walk and drawing attention to myself so I remained where I was. When the driver got back on he walked down the aisle and did a head count to ensure he was not leaving anyone behind. He glanced in my direction and I was sure could not fail to notice the ruined seat next to me, not to mention the state of my clothes but he continued on without comment or change of expression. I had, before this, considered leaving a tip to recompense for the mess but decided in the face of his lack of concern, I would not bother.

After another hour we pulled into the little port town of Essaouira which was constructed in 1760 and originally called Mogador. The walled medina was considered so picturesque that it was added to UNESCO's World Heritage list in 2001. When I had read my guidebook's description I had seen a chance for peace out of the big cities but I had also hoped for artistic inspiration.

When I arrived however, inspiration and painting were the last things on my mind. I staggered off the bus, my head down, embarrassed at how I must look and reclaimed my bags. A woman and young boy came up and tried to interest me in their affordable nearby hotel, 'with shower,' they kept repeating. I would have loved to have gone with them but had already arranged to meet Adrian at a specific hotel in the medina. I hired a young man with a cart to carry my bags because there was no driving traffic allowed in the medina. Normally, I would have loved this bit of information because it meant the hotels would be quieter and rooms free of exhaust from passing traffic. Now however this meant I would have to stagger through the streets in my soiled clothes, hoping I could make it before I became too sick to walk again.

Consulting my way with the tiny map in my guidebook I made my way through the medina gates and into the fringes of the bazaar. People, animals, carts, and bicycles choked the narrow roads and my eyes blurred under the visual assault. I struggled to keep my eyes directed above, checking the roofline for a sign advertising my hotel. At last I saw it and breathing a sigh of relief walked in and up to the front desk.

"Please, do you have any rooms for two people?

The woman behind the desk looked up at me without seeming to see me then back down with a distracted air. "I have only two rooms left but you may choose." She pushed two sets of keys across to me and I trudged up several flights of stairs. With a sinking sensation I noticed neither one had the required TV or air-conditioning but there was no help for it. I had no reserves of energy left to take back to the streets. I chose the room with the most light and dropping off my bag, made my way back downstairs.

"My... husband will be arriving later, his name is Adrian. If you can tell him my room number when he arrives." I closed my eyes feeling a wave of dizziness descend. "I'm sorry," I whispered. "I am quite sick."

Her eyes grew wide as she seemed to notice the front of my shirt for the first time. "Ah! Baby!"

"No, I think something I ate," I said but casting my mind back could not remember anything besides bottled water and a few fried crepes.

"Ah, I can see in your face, it is baby, I sense these things, you will see. No problem, you are not well, we will speak more tomorrow. Trust me, I know," she nodded wisely at me and turning bellowed a man's name. I stood weaving in place and exhausted, decided it didn't really matter if the entire hotel thought I was newly pregnant. All I wanted was to make it into bed before I collapsed. My mother had loaned me her wedding ring for the trip because we had both thought it would be safer for me to pretend I was married while traveling. I had not quite anticipated being accused of pregnancy however. Glancing back at my face she howled again and this time a man came down the stairs with a resigned air as he picked up my second bag.

Once in my room I peeled off my clothes and staggered to the shower only to realize as I tried to turn on the water that the hotel was completely out. Not even a trickle emerged from the taps, hot or otherwise. I could almost hear Adrian grumbling and though the thought of him made me smile, I wished I had the strength to find a different hotel.

Though it was warm, I couldn't stop shivering and wrapped myself in the wool blankets covering the bed. After a couple hours my head pulsing and at the same time feeling light enough to float off of my shoulders, I crept out to find an internet cafe. I staggered through the streets which were lined by an open market selling fruits, vegetables, fresh pastries, and unfortunately a rank smelling table piled high with bloody goat heads, the table next to it had a stack of their little legs. I swallowed hard, held my breath, and averted my eyes as I struggled to keep walking. I managed to use the internet but got no farther and stumbled back to my hotel to spend the rest of the day in bed.

I slept the afternoon and evening away waking briefly to drink water and sprite. When the light of morning began to brighten the room, I woke and lay still. My body felt weak and uncertain and I was afraid to move so I studied the way the light changed on the ceiling, banishing shadows to their daytime resting places and listened to the sound of the market as it began to open outside my open windows.

From outside came the cry of gulls and a hint of the briny tang of ocean drifted in and curled around the room, lazy as a cat. Though I could not see the water from my window, I could picture it in my mind stretching off to the horizon. Years ago when I worked on a cruise ship as a waitress, I fell asleep each night to the slap of the ocean against the hull and the rhythmic movement of my bunk. In the dark, early morning hours, while I set the tables for breakfast, I would watch the sun rise up over the edge of the world, emerging from the water in lines of liquid light. I never got tired of watching it emerge and later set, each one the same and yet completely unique. When I was too busy to catch that singular moment of the sun cresting the horizon, I would feel a loss, as though I had missed something which would never be seen again.

In my off time I used to run on a treadmill in the crew workout room that was set directly in front of a floor to ceiling window. When the sea was rough and the ship pitched with violence or even resting still, at dock, I would run with that limitless horizon in front of me. It was a view that was always transforming and yet always the same: hypnotizing, mesmerizing, eternal. I felt if I could only lose myself in counting the swells of water and regulating my breath to match them, I would break through an invisible layer.

I could understand how a person could become addicted to living on the water, in spite of the work, the unpredictability, the sense of helplessness to its whims and caprices. Laying in my bunk each night was a full surrender, knowing I had no control over the pilot navigating the boat through the perilous rock channels. The water tight doors were sealed when the ship was underway, which ensured if one compartment flooded, the others would not. I knew however, two flights below the water line, if it was my compartment, I would have very little time to make my way in the dark and with the cacophony of alarms screaming, to the stairwell before drowning. Perhaps that surrender to fate was only more evident at sea, where man's helplessness has an immediate presence and clarity. Yet the greatest illusion on land, is the perception of control, which at the whim of unseen forces is blown away, as substantial as dissipating smoke.

"He was a seaman, but he was a wanderer too, while most seamen lead, if one may so express it, a sedentary life. Their minds are of the stay-at-home order, and their home is always with them- the ship; and so is their country- the sea. One ship is very much like another, and the sea is always the same. In the immutability of their surroundings the foreign shores, the foreign faces, the changing immensity of life, glide past, veiled not by a sense of mystery but by a slightly disdainful ignorance; for there is nothing mysterious to a seaman unless it be the sea itself, which is the mistress of his existence and as inscrutable as Destiny."

-Joseph Conrad, Heart of Darkness

There was a definite magic to waking in a new port. Looking out of portholes to see a new dock, sudden mountains arising from the water, where the night before there had been none. There had been a few free afternoons when I had been able to retreat to the highest deck, deck fourteen which was not much more than a platform for the crew to smoke on, in an effort to paint.

I remembered being docked at port, lush hills and cliffs soaring in a combination of black volcanic rock and dizzying green. The mist which wreathed the tops of the peaks eventually rolled down and turned into rain. I had stuck it out as long as I could, painting fast, hunching my body over my canvas in an effort to protect it. Finally I had to stuff my art supplies into my bag and run for the stairway hatch in a thickening downpour. Trying to paint the islands and sky of Hawaii had been like trying to copy a huge mural, the masterwork of an immortal artist. Impossible, but I couldn't help but try in an effort to understand it, capture it, hold onto it with something more tangible than memory.

A Roman Thermal Bath at Midnight

11/14-12/10

The other night, an Italian friend picked me and a friend up to take us on an adventure. It was a long, dark drive and he drove in the middle of the road keeping the dividing line between his wheels while the Italian singer Vasco Rossi growled out lyrics in a whiskey and smoke roughened voice from the speakers. An hour later, somewhere outside of Sienna, we stopped in what seemed like the middle of nowhere. In the darkness we felt our way down an almost invisible trail, tripping over tree roots, and rocks. I followed the lead of the others and shed my clothes before climbing down an embankment. The dirt became slick glowing white stone worn smooth by the passage of hot fragrant water which poured out of large pipes. Clouds of steam filled the air and all around us were naturally forming basins full of sulfur scented water. They were small and numerous enough that each of us could sit in our own bath.

As my body settled into the natural hollows and grooves of the stone and the water rose to my chin, cold bottles of water and peeled segments of oranges were handed around. The best, he taught us, was to sit under the pipes and let the hottest water cascade over your head, down your shoulders, beating and pounding against your skin until your pulse sped up and became so loud that it drowned out everything else. Only then, when the heat of your body had reached its peak should you slip down the smooth rock bank and into the river. The river was still and shallow, rising only to the waist, and the bottom was lined with smooth stones.

When I slid into the cool water, the first time, I almost stopped breathing it was such a shock. By the bank there were natural forming underwater stone ledges and I found I could sit on one still partially submerged in the river and leaning back against the bank, hot water would pour down over my shoulders and back.

By moonlight I could see an outline of crumbling Roman walls and arches that still towered through the trees. There were other people there, all Italian, all silent and through the steam only to be located by the orange gleam of cigarette embers. It was a place shrouded in mystery, even now I could never find my way back. After hours, which passed in a dream, we each took one last dip in the river before scrambling back up the bank to our clothes. The car was more subdued on the ride back, the scent of sulfur rose off our bodies and my skin seemed to hum with the memory of water pounding against it. Later when I got back to my apartment I realized I had grabbed the wrong towel by the side of the river and was now in possession of an orange flowered one. I wonder which one of the Italians there got my towel?

* * *

My roommates and I were walking to school this morning, trying to hurry because we were running late. In front of us a well-dressed lady came out of a shop, got on her bike and was about to ride off when the iron bar that connects the handlebars to the front wheel suddenly snapped. She fell, striking her chin on first the spokes of her front wheel then on the cobblestones. She was bleeding everywhere and her legs were all tangled up in her brake lines. We ran forward and I tried to offer some Kleenex from my bag, but she was so stunned she could barely move. The fall had knocked the breath right out of her. All of the shop owners came out and were fussing over her. Italians are very kind when it comes to a crisis. We managed to help her out of the street and drug the remains of her bicycle to the sidewalk. I got to school late with blood all over my hands. It was scary, her bike looked perfectly fine, and I would never have guessed the metal was ready to go. I am definitely not getting a bike here.

I have, with some effort, been standing up for myself at school. There is a girl here, who went for three years to that same Art Institute in California I went to. She never smiles and always looks as though she just ate something unpleasant. The other day in the morning drawing class, we began a new drawing with a new pose and model. Second year students get to pick their easel positions first, then we go in alphabetical order to divide up the remaining easels. I was second to last to pick and every easel was taken by the time they got to me. I had to go grab an extra easel and try to fit it into any space remaining. One of the best locations had a smidge of space next to it and the instructor made everyone move their easels a couple inches so I could squeeze in. Sure enough, the California girl pipes up, "My name was called before hers, and I would have liked to have had that spot. Why should she be allowed to make everyone move and get to squeeze in wherever she likes? I don't think it's fair."

I felt like snarling at her, "Life isn't fair! Get used to it!" but stayed quiet. The teacher told her, "Well, it's a large class and we have to find a way to accommodate everyone." The funny thing was, I actually preferred where her easel was because I thought it was a better angle, plus in my position every time I backed up I bumped into someone else.

I went up to her a few minutes later and said we could switch places if she liked. Well, she liked that a lot even though she insists on pronouncing my name 'Deedree' and didn't even bother to say 'thank you.' I switched easels with her, got my drawing space all set up and marked down when she flounced back over five minutes later. Everything was all set, class had started and she says, "It is too cramped over there, I want my old spot back."

I stared at her and asked, "Are you serious?"

She stuck her nose in the air, not even apologizing, and said, "Yes."

I shrugged and said, "I'm sorry, I don't want to switch back, you will just have to figure something out." Her little mouth dropped open like a fish and off she stomped. This pose is for four and a half weeks and I will be hanged if I am going to switch back again. I have got a really good spot now too.

My day actually did not start very well, I had mapped in a bunch of reference points for the cast drawing I am starting, hadn't even begun on the line work and had the misfortune of that being the exact instant one of the head instructors showed up to give me my critique. She stared at all the little reference dots and no lines on my sheet of paper and started laughing. It was not nice laughter, you know the kind you can join in on, but really vicious and mocking. I could feel my face turning red and I tried to explain I had just started but she gave me the most disdainful look you can imagine and told me what I had wasn't a drawing and wasn't the way to start a drawing, then walked off. They told us to start with reference points! To ensure the drawing is properly sight size and matches with the cast alongside it, same height, same size, etc. I was pretty mad, embarrassed, and everyone around me kept shooting me these sympathetic looks. Of course, that instructor is legendary for making students cry. I didn't feel like crying, I felt like hitting something, but I wasn't going to let her get the better of me and went back to work.

I had just started again when I caught movement out of the corner of my eye. I turned and there sprawled on top of my jacket, in all of his extremely fat, tomcat glory was the black and white puss who we have all affectionately dubbed Sumo. He looks a bit like a sumo wrestler, being probably one of the best fed cats in Italy as well as having survived and emerged victorious from the rooftop cat brawl. I was pleased that he chose my chair to take a bath on and showered him with affection, instantly cheering up. Nothing like a large cat to put you in a good mood. We draw with plumb lines here, strings with a weight attached to the end which are used to check reference points on a drawing, and we discovered they also make good cat toys.

* * *

I made the cast for my sculpture today, it took me eight hours. In the earlier classes I sculpted a skull out of clay, then while observing the model, I sculpted his profile over the top of the skull. Then I filled in, constantly circling the model, changing the angle in order for every section of the sculpture to develop at the same rate.

When the clay sculpture was done I created a mold by covering the clay with plaster until there was a good even layer. Then on top, for strength, I layered strips of burlap soaked in plaster. Later, when the plaster was dry, I split the mold open and dug out the clay and so, in the end, the original clay sculpture was destroyed in order to make the mold. After the mold was carefully washed, I joined the two halves of the mold together and sealed the seam. Then plaster was poured inside and the mold was continuously rotated by hand so the inside became evenly coated, without air bubbles. When a thick solid layer of plaster had been built up inside the mold,

I stuffed more burlap in the hollow. The next session, using chisels, I cracked off the mold, being careful not to gouge too deep and destroy the plaster cast inside. When I was done chipping off the outer mold I had a copy of my clay sculpture in plaster, which is what is called a cast. It is a lot of work but a very exciting process.

I have hired one of the sculpture students from the school to sit as a portrait model for me at home. He is from South Africa and looks like one of the young soldiers that the famous Spanish painter, Velasquez liked to paint. His curly brown hair falls to his shoulders and he has very deep, melancholy eyes. He came to my apartment on Sunday and posed for three hours until the sun set and I could no longer see.

It has been a long weekend. One of the girls at school was throwing a Thanksgiving dinner and I collected the people she didn't invite and turned it into a poker night. My two roommates and four other girls from school came over. Three people brought wine because they all wanted to bring something but no one wanted to stand in line at the market. Yet, among the seven of us, we only managed to drink one bottle. We served dark chocolate, pizza, spaghetti, and one of the girls brought fresh bread and honey. We bet with toothpicks when we were playing poker and played quite badly because we couldn't remember all of the rules. The deck of cards we used was an art deck I had bought at the Louvre that has a different painting printed on each card. It was fun and made everyone feel less homesick.

You know how I always talk about how everyone drives crazy here, but I never see an accident? Well, I saw my first accident last night. I was walking with two friends to a party, our streetlight was green and we were just about to step off the curb and cross when a speeding scooter tried to turn in front of a car, who had the green light, and was broadsided.

The scooter literally exploded into about three or four different pieces, we almost got hit by flying plastic. The gas tank of the scooter was completely detached and sat in the middle of the intersection spraying petrol in every direction. I was looking frantically around for the driver of the scooter and finally saw her, she had been thrown clear across the road onto the sidewalk where she lay face down unmoving. She had been hit so hard that one of her shoes had been knocked clean off her foot. We started towards her but an officer took charge. I saw her lift her head so she was alive, thank goodness, but it all happened so fast I don't even remember seeing a collision, only the pieces of the scooter flying in all directions. Oh, and she wasn't wearing a helmet.

* * *

I am thinking of going to a different school. I went to the Charles Cecil Studio today and spoke to the director and showed him examples of my work. He is a strange guy, when I introduced myself he said, "Ah, I was in love with a Deirdre once." I wasn't quite sure what to say to that. Later I visited the John Angel Academy and spoke to the secretary. They are in the midst of making a new brochure and application so I am going to check back in a few weeks. The Florence Academy is okay, it's just that I don't want to spend an entire year doing cast drawings when I already spent two years drawing them in Utah. Then at the end of the year, if I am lucky they will allow me to do a cast painting, something I have also already done. I have seen some of the paintings that come out of this school and they are not to my taste. I liked the paintings coming out of the Charles Cecil Studio better and their curriculum moves faster. The Florence Academy has by far the best drawing program of any of the schools in the city, but I am ready to move on. I am also tempted to forget the schools entirely and spend the rest of my time in Italy traveling and painting. Only time will tell. I hope everything is well there, I will write again soon.

Chapter 5

Essaouira: Love and Goodbyes

"Was my load heavy on my shoulders? Were its rough straps cutting my flesh? Indeed they were! I felt it later, but at that moment I was not aware of it. I was aware of nothing.
I knocked myself against sharp rocks, I tore my hands and my face in the thorny bushes.
I was dead to all sensation, stiffened, hypnotized by the will to succeed."
–Alexandra David-Neel, My Journey to Lhasa

9/17/07

I watched Adrian cross the darkened hotel room, an insubstantial phantom until he stood above me his features slowly resolving, "Honey? Are you okay?"

I woke up with a rush and sat up in bed, the morning light was streaming in through the window. I was alone. My shoulders slumped in disappointment, I knew I couldn't expect him before evening but it hadn't kept me from wishing him to appear sooner. I got up gingerly, I was sticky with sleep and sweat but my headache was gone. I had the strength to straighten my room and when I experimentally turned on the sink I was grateful to see a stream of water come out. I scrubbed my filthy clothes and then took a shower.

I summoned the energy to get dressed then slowly crept up the stairs to the rooftop verandah. Breakfast was being served at a handful of tables sheltered under blue cloth umbrellas and a panoramic view of the surrounding medina stretched out in all directions. I tried to enjoy the sight as I struggled to force down mint tea, orange juice and a few pieces of dry bread but each time I reached for my cup my hand shook. My body still felt fragile and uncertain, and I decided to spend the day lying down.

Back in my room I couldn't sleep, I lay in bed and listened to the sounds of the surrounding market, lost in thought. I wasn't afraid anymore. For the longest time I had been ruled by my fear of something going wrong while I was traveling alone. Being sick and stranded in a country where I couldn't speak the language had always been one of my largest concerns. But I didn't feel stranded and I was as sick as any of the times I had been food poisoned as a child traveling in Mexico with my family. One of my worst fears had been realized and I was fine. I was coping with it. If I didn't get better I would simply have the front desk call a doctor. Yet, part of me knew, I was going to be all right.

Watching the light from the window make shadow shapes across the ceiling I tried to remember how traveling had first begun to sink into my blood. As a kid being dragged along to Mexico every year with my parents for vacation, I had grown up eating strange foods, hearing different languages, being exposed to new cultures but I hadn't always enjoyed it. When my father had first come to the United States he had been taken in by two Berkley professors, Lauramay and Everett, in the San Francisco bay area. They had given him somewhere to stay and helped him get through school. When I was young and we would visit I was captivated by a map of the world they had in a back room which was covered with pins labeling all of the countries they had visited. They used to give slide shows of treks through Africa, adventures in South America, excursions across Europe. Their house was always full of visitors, generally former or current Berkeley students, scientists, dancers, writers, and a variety of intellectuals. However, I still found a way to be bored, their board games were outdated, their shelves of books covered science, philosophy, botany, classical music, and literature but seemed lacking in the children's paperbacks I wanted to read. The bathroom was haunted by huge gossamer spider webs lurking in corners and under the sink, inhabited by equally large arachnids that I was not allowed to kill or relocate because Lauramay insisted they kept the flies in check. After awhile on our visits I had gotten used to soft boiled eggs for breakfast with a dash of soy sauce, ripe persimmons bursting out of their skins for dessert and mismatching napkin rings that were reserved for specific people.

When Lauramay died following Everett, she was in her 90s and I was in my second year of college. I had sat with the phone pressed to my ear, listening to my mother's voice and my first emotion had been jealousy. A gut clenching envy that burned through my veins like fire. She had explored the world, she had met and helped countless people. She had never lived her life by halves but instead was a blazing fire in a world often filled with small, briefly struck matches. I wanted that to be my life. I didn't want to finish my bachelor's degree in English and get some boring stable job that would enable me to live a safe, normal life. I wanted my life to be unpredictable, unconventional, exhilarating. In a way, her death changed my life more than any impact she had on me when she was still alive. She had left me a little money for school because she had thought, based on seeing a few of my sketches from high school, that I should pursue my art. She had believed in me, and somehow through her, I was able to believe in myself.

I knew being an artist was never going to be easy. It meant taking a certain amount of life on faith. Faith that things would fall into place, faith that what I was pursuing for my life was worthwhile and had value. Being an artist was all consuming, it took all of my time and concentration. It was selfish of my focus and when I was absorbed in my work I knew I had no time for anyone or anything else. Art settled for nothing less. It was an addiction that once fully succumbed to would never leave the system. I could only push painting aside for short periods of time and even then it would haunt me like a neglected lover, tingling up my hands in a tickling burn and reordering my vision. Without art I became listless, moody, and depressed, unable to take full enjoyment in anything.

As I laid in bed I tried to analyze my work up to date. The paintings I had completed in Mexico were primarily of buildings, hallways, rooms, ruins, arches, and landscapes. Of those paintings only one had a person in it, a semi-successful full figure of a Tarahumaran man. Of the paintings I had completed in Morocco, two portraits and two that were more architectural, the portraits were more captivating. I was not sure if it was because they were of a person and images with people are always more immediately interesting because the human viewer can identify with the subject. Or, if it was because I enjoyed painting people more than any other subject and this bled through onto the canvas.

With the portrait, I was forced to pay more attention to detail, color, light, and tone, because the smallest mistake in the placement of an eye, curve of the mouth and vast distortions resulted. Yet it was more than that, more than the technical focus, there was the emotional side, the interaction with the model even if it was silent. Even the best, most detached model radiated an awareness of the artist and attempted to supply what they felt was asked for, expected, needed. The strongest exchange always came later however, a good hour into the session, after the pose had melted from a stiff, self-consciousness into a languid natural gesture. The veil of formality is cast aside. There is an unspoken vulnerability, not only on the part of the model who gives but on the part of the artist who receives.

"She had found that the relationship with her subjects
could be as intense as that between lovers,
or even a doctor and patient. A portrait was a
continuous intimate struggle between observation
and secrecy, and there was no protection
from the artist's gaze."
–Jody Shields, The Crimson Portrait

I was interrupted from my thoughts by a loud knock at the door. As I struggled to get up and into pants, wondering if it was the hotel staff checking to make sure I was still alive, the knock came again, then again. Each time it sounded slightly more annoyed and impatient. I stumbled as I hopped across the room trying to zip up my pants. When I opened the door and peered around it, Adrian filled the doorway, sweaty, blue eyes blazing. He glanced at me briefly, before his eyes flickered over my shoulder to take in the room.

"Where is the AC? The television?" he demanded as he threw down his backpack and flopped down on the bed. "Do you know what it took to get here? I had to bail my taxi driver out of jail!"

I closed the door with a sigh but could not help but smile as I made my way back to the bed to sit down. "I've been sick you know. This was the most expensive, swank hotel listed by my budget guidebook and I'm sorry if I didn't have the strength to go searching the town when I saw it wouldn't meet your minimum requirements." I paused, "It's good to see you."

"Yeah? Well... it's good to see you too. I got your email, I know you've been sick. I was worried. Why do you think I got here so fast? I could have waited around and taken the late bus from Casablanca but I chose to spend 200 bucks on a private taxi to take me directly here. It was a decent enough plan until he was stopped halfway here for speeding and it only happened to be his fifth offense so the police put him in the back of their car in handcuffs. So there I was right? I swear, things like this only happen to me, and I'm asking them, 'what am I supposed to do now?' I'm standing around trying to flag down anyone really, when this taxi stopped, stuffed with people and they offered me a ride on the roof. Literally on the roof. I couldn't believe it. I was like, 'no way in hell.' Then this smartass kid walks up and offers me a ride and I agree. Get this, when he comes back fifteen minutes later it's with a donkey and cart." Adrian shook his head.

"All this time the police have been laughing at me and filling out paperwork on my taxi driver, the speed demon. So I say to them, 'how much is it going to cost to get you guys to let this guy drive me to Essaouira?' So they say they want a hundred bucks, I pay it and then we are on our way. We get here with no more problems, he drops me off and then I realize my girlfriend," he stopped to glare. "Sent me some wacked out directions to get to this hotel and I got completely lost. I have been wandering the streets of this damn town for the last...hour."

I rolled my eyes; in Adrian-speak that probably translated to about twenty minutes. "I gave you directions for the entrance the buses drop you by, not the entrance the private taxis drop you by. I didn't realize you were coming that way, I'm not psychic you know. Hey! I'm sick aren't you supposed to be fussing over me... or something?"

"That was before. Now I'm tired, grumpy, and starving, let's go get something to eat."

I stood up experimentally, the room didn't swim, the nausea did not return. I felt light headed and weak but that could also be the effect of eating so little. "Come on," I said. "Let's go find you something."

"Actually that story is nothing, after I left you in Marrakesh to catch my plane in Casablanca for Guinea... now there was a crazy adventure!" I closed the door behind us and we started down the stairs. "So there I was in Marrakesh, I found my train to Casablanca, no problem, found my first class car, got my bags all stowed. Still, I had like fifteen minutes before we were supposed to leave and I was starving. So I went up to the porter and asked him if I had enough time to get off and buy something to eat and he said I did and that he would keep an eye on my bags. I went to this little nearby snack kiosk, you know the ones, they sell soda and stuff. I was buying this loaf of bread and there was this whole deal because the guy didn't have change for my bill but I didn't have anything smaller. You know how it is."

I did, in Mexico as well as Morocco trying to break the bills the ATM machines dished out was next to impossible. "All of a sudden the train whistle went off, so I started getting impatient but the guy was still scrabbling around looking for change. Then my train started to move, so I yelled at him to forget the change and I started running. I mean, it was more than me missing my train, the last one to Casablanca and missing my flight. My bags were on the train, leaving without me. So there I was, running as fast as I could, and the train was speeding up and then there was the porter holding his hand out to me from the last car. It was just like a movie. This whole time I couldn't believe this was happening. I was just running my guts out. He pulled me up at the last minute and I made it, but" he chuckled and shook his head, "it doesn't stop there."

I shot him a look as I weaved around a small man who had stopped his cart in the middle of the street. "So then, the train had been traveling for awhile, maybe an hour or so, when the lights went out and the car started to slow down, then stopped moving altogether. I got up to check the situation out and found the porter looking out the window at receding lights. He said it was no big deal, happened all the time, our car had become detached from the rest of the train and sooner or later the train would figure it out and return to hook back up with us. Then we would be underway again. The only problem would be if another train came along in the dark before our train came back, because they could potentially hit us since we didn't have any power for lights. I was like, 'Great. You have got to be kidding me.' We waited an hour, then the train came back hooked up and we were underway again. Hey, let's eat here."

I pulled out a plastic chair at the small street café and took a laminated menu from the waiter's hand. "So we got to Casablanca late and the whole station was already closed for the night. I mean lights out, locked up tight as a drum. To get out to the parking lot we had to climb over this padlocked gate, I even had to help these tourist women throw their bags over. By the time I got to the other side there was only one taxi left and he was trying to triple the normal fare to take me to the airport. I negotiated him down and thought everything was settled until he stopped in the middle of this really bad neighborhood. I mean really, really not where you wanted to be late at night. There was no other traffic. He told me I could agree to pay his fare or he was going to leave me there. I was so mad, you have no idea. When we finally pulled up to the airport I was tempted not to pay him. You would have been proud of me though; I held my temper because I realized the whole situation wasn't worth it. I'll have a cheese pizza." I looked up at the waiter and ordered some noodles with red sauce. I figured I would eat what I could and if I relapsed, Adrian would hopefully take care of me.

"That wasn't even the end of it. Then I got into the airport only to find out they were closing until morning and I was not allowed to stay in the airport until a few hours before my early morning flight. There was no way at this point I was going to try to take another taxi to a hotel, I wouldn't have had enough time to sleep for it to have been worth it anyway." Adrian took a swallow from his water bottle.

"Well?" I asked impatiently, "What did you do?"

"You are going to love this. I went outside and huddled on the pavement with my back to the wall and tried to sleep. It was freezing and I felt like a homeless person. I woke up an hour later and I swear, every stray cat in the area was huddled up against me for warmth."

I snorted, "Actually that doesn't surprise me one bit. You are a walking heater. You weren't mean to them were you? You didn't shoo them away? They were cold."

Adrian sighed loudly, "No I wasn't mean to them, damn cats. I knew if I was, my girlfriend would get mad. How have you been doing? How was painting?" As I began to tell him I realized I was glad, more glad then I could have imagined, to have him with me again. I didn't want to be sick and alone, I wanted someone around who would push me out of it, force me to keep up. With Adrian there would be no time for being sick.

* * *

After breakfast on the hotel terrace the next morning we walked around town looking for a different hotel. We finally found one to his liking just down the street. A strong ocean breeze came in through the windows to keep the room cool and there was a TV showing an American movie marathon in English for the entire month of Ramadan. Strangely enough the room cost less than the one I had been in.

We headed to the beach after switching hotels. There were few people out, though the sun was blazing and we nearly had the area to ourselves. Adrian left me relaxing in the shade of a thatched umbrella on a rented lawn chair and went to test the water, which he found to be too cold for swimming and with a vicious undertow according to locals. We wandered down to the docks where brightly painted wooden fishing boats were tied. Large piles of fishing net lay out and groups of fishermen sat relaxing and talking.

We paid to walk on the Skala du Port, an impressive sea bastion with views over the fishing port and across the water to the Ile de Mogador. The Ile de Mogador was part of a grouping of islands once called Iles Purpuraires for the purple imperial cloth the Romans once produced there. Now they were a nature preserve for birds and were not open to the public without a permit. The Ile de Mogador was flanked on either side by a fort which, combined with the fort on the mainland, covered all approaches to the bay. The ramparts we were walking on were lined with a large 17th century collection of European canons presented to Sultan Sidi Mohammed ben Abdallah by ambitious merchants.

As I took pictures of Adrian I studied my surroundings, the angles, the textures of rock and sky, the slant of the sun, the number of people walking by, the proximity of swooping seagulls and the strength of the ocean breeze, trying to gauge the potential for a painting. As we walked I still felt waves of dizziness left over from being sick but I was curious about the town I had seen so little of. I not only wanted to find painting subjects but I wanted to take advantage of my last days with Adrian. When he left Morocco this time, it would be to head back to the United States for training for his deployment to Afghanistan. I wouldn't be joining up with him. I didn't know when we would see each other again.

I pushed my thoughts away and concentrated on my surroundings. Unlike Taroudannt, I could immediately see a lot of potential painting subjects: endless narrow winding streets, whitewashed houses with blue trim set with heavy antique wood doors, colorful shops with tables of wares glinting outside, and rugs hanging down the length of alleys. The entire town was chock full of art galleries; paintings of upturned blue boats resting on the shore and seagulls wheeling above the medina walls, were everywhere. I realized I would have to be careful when choosing my location. The sun above was strong, I would not be able to stand painting in it for long periods of time and the ocean breeze was variable, at times gentle and cooling, at other times gusting strong enough to tip over a painting easel.

We walked a little more in the evening and found the streets changed after dark. Some places closed, others opened and quite a few young men whispered to Adrian, 'Hashish? Hashish?" as he passed by smoking his cigar.

When we arrived back at the hotel he breathed a sigh of relief, "Man, if one more person offers me drugs while I am here I swear I am going to lose it. Promise me you will try not to go out after dark when I am gone. "

I hugged him, "That's an easy promise."

* * *

We spent the next day exploring side streets and shops we had not seen before as he bought a few last minute items. We found the shopkeepers much less rabid and tenacious then the Marrakesh ones and that it was possible to ask how much something cost without fear of having one's pockets emptied and clothes bartered. Adrian discovered a sort of minimarket selling all sorts of fancy cheeses and breads, which we bought a selection of along with yoghurt, fruit juices, chocolate cookies and fudge squares to take back to our room for snacks.

As we walked out of the shop we passed a young European woman dressed in a thin sleeveless top with no bra beneath. I barely noticed until a Moroccan man passing us hissed something venomously in Arabic. Adrian's head came up with a snap and he turned to stare behind us at the man who was disappearing around the corner. "What did he say?" I asked, still shocked by the expression on his face.

"He called her a whore," Adrian said softly. We looked back at the young woman who stood oblivious having paused to look in a shop window. Every contour of her breasts was clearly outlined as the wind moved the cloth close to her body. I nervously readjusted the long sleeves of my loose shirt. Adrian's eyes flicked down to me and a ghost of a smile touched his mouth, "you are fine, trust me."

We rounded a corner and walked up a stone ramp to the Skala de la Ville, another sea bastion, which ran along the northern cliffs. Beneath the bastion were a group of marquetry and wood carving workshops that worked with thuya wood, a mahogany-like hardwood from a local coniferous tree. The craftsmen used both the trunk and roots, and claimed their work to be the best in the country. The spicy smell of fresh sawdust was intoxicating enough to pull anyone off of the street and I found myself unable to keep from walking into each one in order to examine possible picture frames for my paintings.

For our last dinner together, Adrian dressed in a fine handmade linen shirt that a shop had custom made for him the night before because all of their shirts were too small in the arms. He bought me a woman's shirt which hung to mid-thigh with slits up each side to the waist and belled out long sleeves. It clashed with my blue plastic flip flops and baggy stained cargo pants but I figured it was the attempt to look presentable that was important. The night before as Adrian had waited for his shirt I had sat at an elegant restaurant across the way and had dessert. I had ordered a small plate of custard and mint tea which was presented in a silver tea pot and poured from a spot by the waiters head clear down to the small glass held at hip height on a little tray. It was then presented with an elegant flourish as though it were a fine vintage French wine. Intrigued I had persuaded Adrian to return with me the next night for dinner.

We had waited until after 8pm to eat but we were still the first patrons to arrive and had our choice of tables. Adrian picked out one in the corner and we sat on stiff silken brocaded couches amidst artfully tossed pillows, a candle burning in the center of the table from a heavy bronze candlestick. After we ordered, silence fell thick and heavy between us. There seemed suddenly little to say. His face appeared distant, his eyes unfocused and I knew he was already thinking of reporting to Kansas, the training, the upcoming deployment.

"I wish I could come with you," I said, I looked down at the tablecloth and picked at a loose thread of embroidery.

"I know, it's just that I won't have an apartment. I will probably have to live on post in either barracks or a hotel for soldiers. Even if I got an apartment I would be leaving in three months and then you would be stuck in Kansas. If we were married..." He smiled at me wryly.

I frowned at the small string I could not keep myself from playing with, "you know how I feel about marriage."

"Not all marriages end in divorce, there are some happily married couples out there. It can work, both people just have to work at it is all. Look," he reached over and took my hand. "It's okay, I just don't want to lose you is all."

"I know, I don't want to lose you either but a wedding ring won't keep someone from leaving if that is what they truly want to do. We are happy as we are, I just don't see why we need to change it."

He sighed, "It would just make it simpler with the military is all. Will you wait for me though?" I nodded and tried not to think of my last long distance relationship and how it had ended in disaster. I tried to focus on the friendship we had and I hoped we were both strong enough. I hoped I was strong enough and that we would be together again someday.

* * *

As I walked with him to the bus station the next morning I thought about the process of parting from someone, whether it was permanent or temporary. How in the days that followed there would be a sense of disconnection. The bond that is created when you are in the other person's company day after day, where communication can be conducted through a quick glance, would start to dissolve as the mind begins to isolate itself again. The hollow ache of something missing, something having been lost, would become by degrees more easily ignored, until the exact tone of their eyes, the timbre of their voice, the tilt of their head in laughter, their hands in gesture are not so easily recalled. The person eventually becomes a sum of memories, two dimensional, a ghost in the mind, whether you want them to or not. In a year from now, we would most likely both be different, and we would have to relearn each other again.

Trying to think back to all of the people I had said goodbye to in the last ten years of constant moving and traveling, it was hard suddenly to pull up each of their faces, the circumstances. They all began to blur into each other after awhile. It was easiest not to hold on, to consider each friendship made as temporary and fleeting, to be savored against the day when it would be gone.

We stood, a small oasis of silence surrounded by the cacophony of the dirt bus lot. It was awkward suddenly. I wasn't sure what was expected of me. It seemed wrong somehow just to hug him and leave. Was I supposed to wait until he was on the bus and it started to pull away? Was I supposed to stand in the middle of the street and hold up traffic in a gesture of abandonment, weeping bitter tears and waving forlornly? I suddenly wanted the whole thing done with, I wanted to retreat to my hotel and get ready for painting.

"Okay, time to say goodbye," he said.

I looked at my wrist at the cheap watch I had picked up in Taroudannt, "But your bus doesn't leave for another-"

"That's okay; just give me a hug and a kiss." As I looked up at him I realized that maybe he didn't want the long drawn out goodbye either, he wanted to move on, focus on the journey ahead of him as well. He pulled me into his arms and I could feel the comfort that I had found in our first embrace, the sense of security, the small whisper of home. "Goodbye honey, be safe, I love you."

I nodded against his chest and whispered, "love you too." Then I turned on my heel and walked away, I didn't trust myself to look back this time. There was a great stillness within me, a silence, as though my body were listening, listening very carefully for the thoughts of my soul. I concentrated on the sun around me, each step I put down on the uneven surfaces of the sidewalk, navigating around carts and people. I focused on the way back to the hotel.

When I got back I pulled out two canvases and taped them to my foam-core travel boards. I stuck a few charcoal sticks for sketching in compositions into my pocket and with one last look around, I left on the hunt. As I lost myself in the maze of alleys, stopping and squinting from time to time to analyze effects of light and architecture, I pushed Adrian to the back of my thoughts. In my nature I had found clarity in duality, with Adrian I was: girlfriend, travel companion, tourist; on my own I was myself: artist, wanderer, explorer.

"To live, one must balance emotion and creation...
It did not mean not loving, not giving one's self.
In balance too, there was the whole giving.
The strong one could make
a whole out of the two portions.
Everything extreme meant death; art had saved me
when I gave too much emotion.
Emotion would save me from too much art."
–Anais Nin

Finally, I found two less used alleyways that seemed to stand out from the rest by some trick of light, some angle of perspective. In an illusion of converging lines, melting angles, colliding surfaces, they were at once similar yet completely different. Each however, held me longer then all of the others and after a few hours of sketching in the outlines of a composition for each one in charcoal on my blank canvas I decided to return the next day and begin painting.

In the second alley one man stopped to peer over my shoulder, chuckled and said, "Oh, you are Van Gogh!" I gave him a distracted smile before returning to my work.

In late afternoon I bought a pizza at one of the cafes and retreated to my hotel room to eat. The setting sun lit the room's maroon curtains on fire as it glowed through the smudged window panes. The turquoise painted walls swam in shadows and the Mediterranean red window sills were edged in a suggestion of dying heat. It was a study in contrasts and I thought if painted correctly it could be a sketch of longing. A glimpse of the setting sun captured only in the illusory flavor of reflections, the effect it had on surroundings, rather than a painting of the sun itself. A window edged in light that hinted at the cool sea air outside, a suggestion of the exotic lines of distant white buildings, the cry of birds echoing off near shores.

The period of time in which the light would be just right however was fleeting, perhaps only 45 minutes before the sun would set completely and the room became submerged in shadow. Still, I was inspired enough that I sketched it out on another canvas and resolved to start on it the next evening. It would be a painting to keep my thoughts busy in the early evenings, distract me from the silence and echoes of a room filled only with the wistful ache of my heart.

Painting Among the Dead

My Dear Family, *6/25/01*

I write you from the tiny hill town of Passignano Sul Trasimeno in Umbria which decorates a hill overlooking a lake. Small cobbled walkways wind up between the buildings in a maze of crumbling stone and hanging vines. Above the town is a ruined stone fort where I sat for a few hours near a half collapsed wall trying to paint a watercolor of the lake. From my vantage point the lake is framed by the remains of a free standing stone doorway that, lacking walls, has an almost spectral quality to it.

In the afternoon I took a ferry across the lake to the main island where there was a small lace museum. I followed a dirt road and discovered an old ruined villa the caretaker let me walk through. Built of stone, the main hall had broken stained glass windows and crumbling water stained frescoes. In the center of the building all of the rooms opened onto a two story high courtyard and from it a crumbling balcony stuck out over the water of the lake. All of the rooms were shuttered; the only light to illuminate them came from the sun peeking through broken slats. Peeling silk wallpaper hung from the walls in strips, a billiard table with filthy green felt rotted away on an uneven floor and one huge room had an antique baby grand piano with keys warped from moisture. What an oil painting it would make! But I am already locked into so many projects I don't know how I could get the time to return.

I guess it won't be a surprise to any of you to hear that after finishing my second trimester at the Florence Academy I left the school and decided to spend my remaining months in Italy working on my own. When I left, I stole one of the school's best female models by promising her more money and no more standing poses, only sitting or reclining, which are a lot easier. She is half Iranian, and half Italian with long dark hair, a wide mouth which is always curving into a languorous smile and bewitching eyes. She is an accomplished dancer and she brings that graceful abandon to her poses. Of course working with models is never as simple as I would like. She showed up the other day after wrecking her scooter, covered in huge bruises. It was the day I was going to start incorporating color over the green and white grisaille under-painting. I was ready to strangle her. Yet, she has such a natural sensuality combined with a cheerful, agreeable nature that it is easy to become inspired by her poses and spend hours in her company.

The other day, after I commented on how difficult it was to find male models, she smiled thoughtfully and told me she might know someone. She knew a man who could use the extra money and she described him as a black belt in karate and absolutely beautiful. She gave him my number and when he called I set up a time for him to come over and start posing. He had never modeled before and didn't speak any English so I knew communication might get tricky.

When he arrived, I had the model stand and my easel all set up and I was busy sharpening pencils for the initial sketch. For privacy, I have been having my models pose in my bedroom using an antique wood chest as a model stand. This had never seemed awkward with female models. Yet, with this unknown man standing in front of me, my room for the first time, felt small and the bed seemed to loom at my back.

He asked if I wanted him to undress and I looked up, distracted and said, "Si, si, va bene." He stripped down to scarlet red briefs and with wide eyes asked, "Tutti?" (everything?)

I glanced up from my paper with a frown, wondering what exactly my other model had told him or forgot to tell him. "Si," I said firmly and getting up demonstrated the sitting pose I wanted him to try on the wood chest. A brief look of near panic crossed his face as he hooked his fingers into the waist band of his underwear. I turned away and ignored him completely, giving him time to breathe as I finished my set up.

Still, he finally hit a pose I liked, sitting with his back to me, knees curled to his chest, which gives his torso an arching curve. He is well muscled yet has retained flexibility and the play of light across his back has potential. By letting him play his own music, giving him a towel to wear on his breaks (he forgot a robe) and not staring at him when he was not modeling, he started to relax and I think by the end was enjoying the novelty of the experience.

Being a model, especially a figurative one, is not easy. To earn a little extra money I have started nude modeling for the Angel Academy's afternoon classes. The Angel Academy is one of the other art schools in town, in competition for foreign students with the Florence Academy. As a model, I have found it is hard to be the right temperature. I am either too cold or too hot and by the time I figure it out, the class has started and it is too late to move and change the setting on the small heater by the model stand. The first time I took my robe off and got in front of the class, was definitely intimidating. The worst that ever happened however, was one afternoon while in a standing pose I started to get light headed and thought for sure I was going to faint. I had to break the pose early in order to go to the bathroom and splash water on my face. I got right back on the stand though and completed the session.

* * *

I have begun a series of paintings up in the San Miniato cemetery, where time takes on a different meaning. It can best be measured in the amount of green moss which has crept up the length of the statues decorating the tombs. I am working on a series of five paintings that feature some of these sculptures, though it was difficult to choose only five. I could easily spend months painting here. The rain weathered and stained marble faces stare lost and blank into the distance, carrying the weight of the family's sorrow in their posture, surrounded as they are by the remains of death. It is as though nature has reclaimed these manmade pieces of art and recreated them by half burying them in dead leaves, a fall of dirt, a blackened smudge submerging pure white marble. I spend all day crouched over canvas, the only noise is the lonely husk of the wind, small cries of birds, the occasional screeches of cats, and the sound my brush makes as it smooths paint onto my canvas.

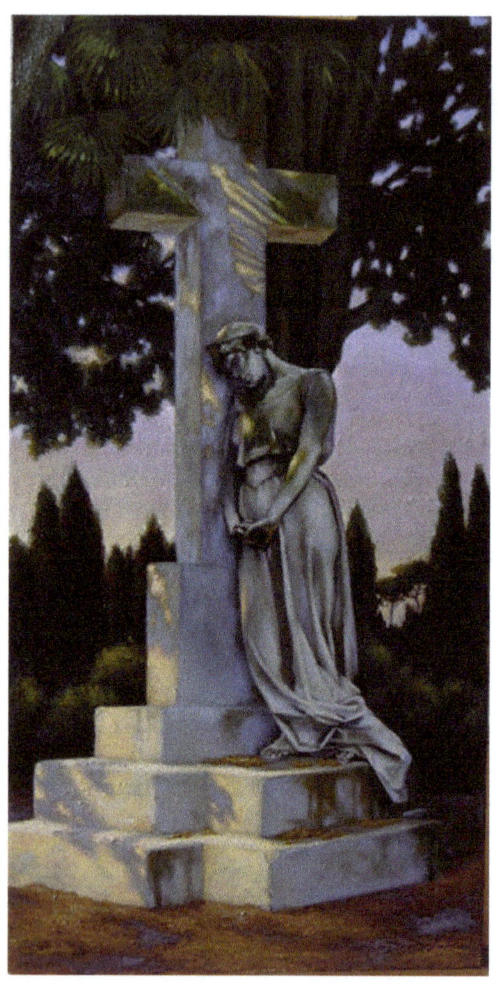

The stray cats are everywhere; there are six or seven fairly young kittens already wild and properly spooky creeping into tombs and sprawling in the shade of crosses and angel wings. The monastery is connected to the church and as I pass beneath it with my paint box and easel, I always look up at the small barred windows hoping to see a monk stare back out,

but they are never there. Sometimes I can hear dishes rattling in the kitchen, but I only see the monks near sunset when their voices rise and fall on the drift of incense, singing vespers in the bowels of the church with its gracefully curving architecture and colorful mosaics. There is a flower shop connected to the library, selling flowers for the graves and the smell of them combines with that of the rose bushes and curls under your nose, heavy as sleep.

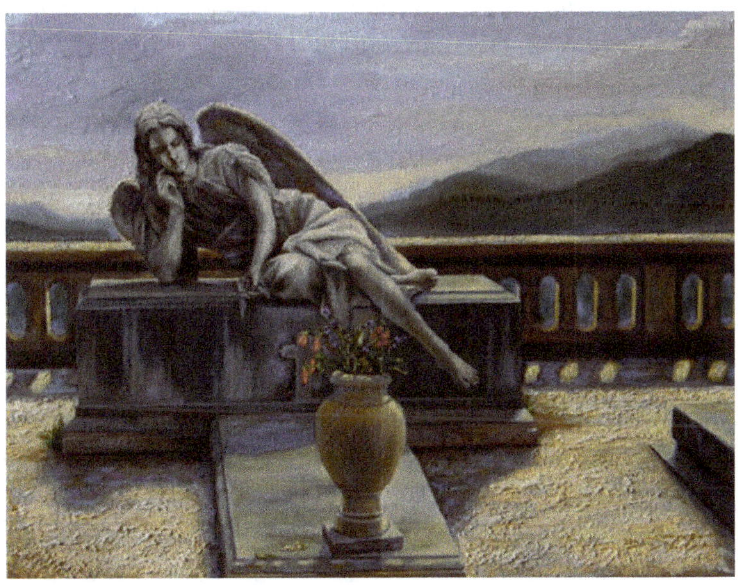

Now that it is summer there are too many insects, tiny green aphids, miniature fruit flies that love to land on my paintings and become immediately stuck. As I try to pry them up their miniature bodies turn into instant corpses, crumpling to unrecognizable black splotches. Small red bites appear on my body and fade, while bees continuously make war on my unprotected head.

I love painting up there but it is not without the occasional annoyance. The other day walking back to my apartment with paint box and easel in hand, next to a stone wall, I heard, "ssssttt!" I looked up and at the top of the wall a guy was standing gesturing to himself with his pants around his ankles. After months of drawing nude models I was pretty unimpressed and without a change in expression or pause in my step I kept walking. Coming toward me were two older Italian women and I heard a rustle and jingle behind me as he hurriedly pulled his pants up and refastened his belt. Lucky for him he was quick enough; otherwise, those Italian ladies would have given him hell. The funny thing is I think he expected some sort of reaction, either positive or negative, but to get none whatsoever, I am sure, was surprising and a little insulting.

The other day there was a huge citywide celebration for the patron saint of Florence. I found a spot on the street curb, still warm from the day's sun, to sit on in the center of a large crowd. Behind me on the banks of the Arno three hot air balloons prepared to rise, bursts of flame spurted from them lighting up the crowd. There was only a sliver of moon but it was large and yellow hanging close to the horizon and over our heads wheeled and swung a handful of careening bats. At ten pm all the lights on the street were turned off and in the dark silence the fireworks came, filling the sky with color, light, and thunder. The cannon blasts were so loud that my teeth rattled and eyes watered. Yet the fireworks that were quieter seemed less popular to the crowd than the ones that arrived with a scream and a bang. The fireworks gave off such an illusion of falling close to earth before disappearing that child and adult alike reached out their hands as if to catch the falling embers...

Chapter 6

Finding the Muse

"Work is love made visible.
And if you cannot work with love
but only with distaste
it is better that you should leave your work
and sit at the gate of the temple
and take alms of those who work with joy.
For if you bake bread with indifference, you bake
a bitter bread that feeds but half man's hunger.
And if you grudge the crushing of grapes,
your grudge distils a poison in the wine
and if you sing though as angels
and love not the singing
you muffle man's ears to the voices of the day
and voices of the night"
–Kahlil Gibran The Prophet

9/21/07

I woke up at 6am and got out of bed quickly before I could give myself time to think about it. I had packed my painting supplies the night before and leaving was as simple as picking them up as I headed out the door. I arrived at the first alley a little worried. I had drawn the composition in the day before using late afternoon light but intended to paint in the morning and was unsure how the light effect might be changed. However, at first glance the light seemed the same and I began to get set up.

I pulled out my camera tripod and screwed my paint box onto the top of it; folding up the lid. I attached my canvas and removed the saran wrap from the oil paint I had squeezed out onto the palette the night before. From my experience painting in Mexico I had decided against bringing a portable stool and instead had brought a portable easel. The camera tripod my paint box screwed onto would enable me to step back from my painting as I worked. I had also disguised my paint medium and thinner in juice and water bottles and they had not been confiscated at the airport.

I had been painting for only half an hour when sunlight began to pour into the alley, blinding me and ruining the indirect, glowing light effect I had been going for. What had also not been present the afternoon before was a strong wind blowing out of an alley to my back, which I realized must extend almost to the ocean-facing medina wall. The cold wet wind that blew directly out of the Atlantic Ocean was called the Gharbi. It constantly rocked my easel and my hands soon went numb from the chill. I lasted however, an hour and a half more until the entire canvas was covered with a layer of paint. I had hoped to work on it for three hours total before shelving it for the day but I couldn't take the wind another minute and ignoring the sunlight had become impossible. I could see, as I removed the canvas, that I had accomplished a subtle effect already. The Gharbi was against me as I gathered my things and it blew my canvas face down on the dirty alley floor twice. By the time I got back to the hotel I could see the paint was embedded with grit.

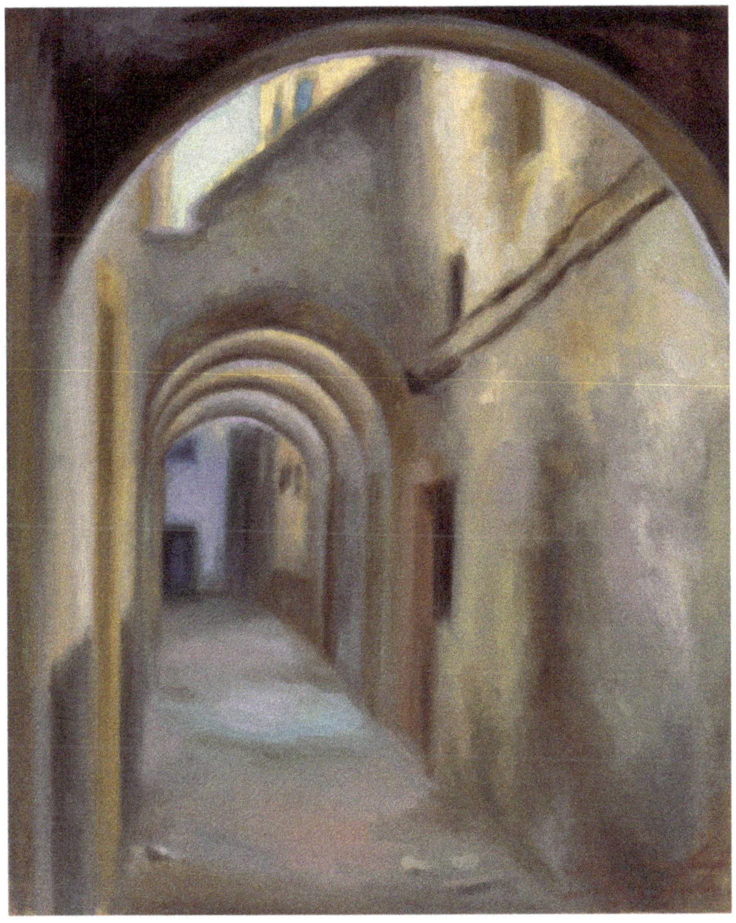

I tried to warm up at a café near my hotel by sitting in the sun with a glass of hot mint tea only to feel thoroughly harassed by a mix of Bryan Adams, Celine Dion, and Elvis Presley which came churning out of their stereo system. By afternoon I was feeling conflicted. I was a little intimidated by my second painting location because it had more open shops near it with young bored salesmen who, I felt sure, would pester me. I got my equipment together and headed out the door. I knew I had to try for it.

When I got to the new alley I was eyed speculatively by a few men leaning against a nearby wall, and perched on stools near open shop doors but I kept my eyes averted and shoulders back, trying to seem confident and sure. As I set up my painting tripod a man observing me said, “Photo? Camera?”

I shook my head and said, “Painting.”

He nodded and said, “Ah yes, you were here the day before.” He watched me a few minutes more, then turned and left. As I began to paint I realized I was going to be left alone, and a small kernel of hope began to unfurl within me. The alley before me held a hint of the bazaar, rugs and bright dresses hung the length of the stone walls, and black iron lanterns jutted out at intervals. Above, connecting the span of the alley like a bridge, was a room with a single blue door which opened to a steep drop. The entire alley was lit with indirect pearlescent light except for at the far end, where sunlight poured through the end of a dark gloomy tunnel. With the whitewashed walls and blue accents, it was a typical Moroccan scene and exactly what I had been seeking.

“Do you mind if I watch?”

I looked up at a Moroccan man who stood a polite distance from me. I shrugged, “Sure.”

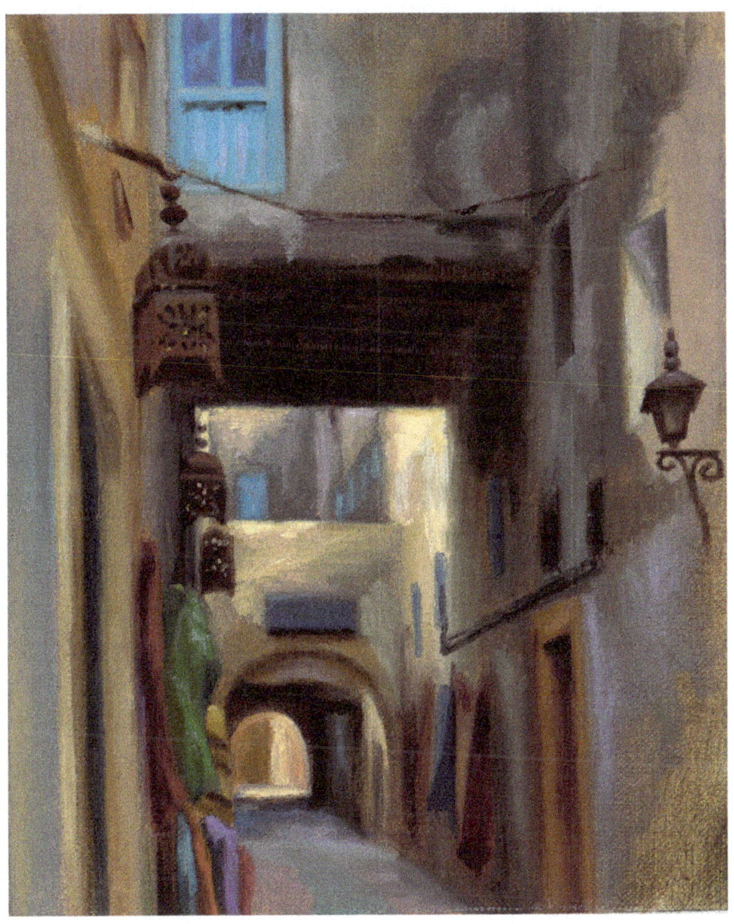

He watched a little while in silence. I felt self-conscious but forced myself to relax, move slowly, deliberately, and to consider each brushstroke. "I work in the art gallery at the end of this alley. I also am a painter but my work is more abstract, modern. I do calligraphy as well. If you need anything, supplies, you should let me know."

I paused and considered him for a moment. His English was some of the best I had yet heard in Morocco. He was obviously well educated. "Actually I need a model, someone local to pose for me... if you know anyone who wants work, wants to make some extra money, it's an easy job." Mentally I flashed back to my own experiences as a model in Italy ten years before, the tedium, the muscle pain, the self-consciousness. It wasn't that easy, but I was hardly looking for a nude model. Sitting for a portrait was far easier.

He nodded slowly as he considered, "I will ask around. Good luck with your work." He raised his hand in a gesture of farewell and walked away.

Time passed, my spot was well sheltered from the sun and wind and I was surprised at how easy it was to focus on the work before me. When I finished for the day I returned to the woodwork shops and at one of them ordered a couple of small frames to be made because they did not have the right size in stock. The smell of the wood was delicious and as I left I could not keep my eyes from lingering on the polished surfaces of handmade tables and chairs. What it must be like to have a home to fill with such things.

* * *

I woke early the next morning impatient to be painting. I ate a roll as I gathered my bags and set out for the windy alley. This time however, I was prepared. I wore a jacket and by arriving an hour earlier, gave myself more time before the sun suffused the scene. Yet, as I set up my tripod I discovered there was no wind, my jacket was unnecessary. In its absence however, the trash pile a little in front of me and to the side reeked with nothing to push its unsavory aromas away. One old man emptied a slop bucket into the drain next to me and it smelled so awful I had to hold my breath to keep from gagging.

The peace of my morning went uninterrupted, few people were out and while a handful came to either add to the trash pile or to pick through it, no one spoke to me. The alley was used mainly as a small secondary foot path but was not well traveled and I liked it for its strange, surreal architecture. There were a series of three archways that split up the length of the passageway, holding up nothing and serving no immediate purpose beyond dividing light and color. Although the alley was filthy it had quaintly painted doors, one pink, another green, this one yellow, that blue. It was hard when painting not to idealize the light and color but to remember to grit it down a little, paint the odd piece of trash, the dangling electrical line, the grungy gaping window, and the smears of green and brown on the patchy white walls. It was important to retain the character, which gave the setting a unique sort of beauty and an added touch of realism.

To some extent, I felt there was only so much that could be done on location. After working on site for up to three hours I liked to let a painting have a breather of half an hour before I looked at it again to analyze. Then, with a fresh eye, I could still quickly blur lines or add emphasis in areas before the paint dried. Painting from instinct or memory was acceptable only after the initial work had been done on location. The preliminary painting was the equivalent of notes taken for a thesis paper; after the initial work had been completed, based off of factual observation, it could later be expanded upon.

That afternoon I returned to the busy alley and finished my painting within the hour. The artist I had met the day before never returned with news of a model so I walked down the alleyway and peeked into his gallery hoping to see him. The gallery was a series of connecting rooms set off of a large sunlit central courtyard featuring everything from paintings and pottery to rugs and antiques. The artist was not there but one of the owners was and intrigued by my alley painting spent a few minutes examining it.

I told him I was looking for a model and asked if he had any suggestions. With a nonchalant shrug, he recommended anyone off the street. Wondering if I was pushing my luck, I asked whether I could paint in his shop. The main problem that had occurred to me was I needed somewhere public to paint, where being disturbed by the public could be kept to a minimum and I did not consider my hotel to be an option. The gallery was huge, more like a converted house and there was plenty of room. The gallery owner shrugged, so long as I was not in the way, no problem. Deep in thought I left and walked back into the alley where I stood for a moment, undecided as to my next move.

“Hello madam, you finish your painting?” I looked up to see the rug salesman across the way walking forward with a smile. He took the painting from me carefully and studied it. “Yes! There, there is my shop, and my rugs, it is very nice work madam. What are you painting now?”

“I’m not sure. I am looking for a model, someone to sit for me. Do you know of anyone who would like to make a little extra money? I would pay.” He tilted his head and gave me a long considering look. A man in a leather jacket sitting in front of his shop reading the newspaper had overheard our conversation because he folded his paper and crossed to us. They looked at each other and consulted in a stream of Arabic.

The man in the leather jacket smiled at me, “My friend Isham would like to pose for you, for two hours here in front of his rug shop. He charges 300 dirham.” I had only paid my model in Taroudannt 120 dirham for three hours and I narrowed my eyes at him.

"Even in my country, models do not cost so much," I said.

"Yes but Isham must run his business, if he closes his store to work for you he will lose customers."

I nodded and gave Isham a look of sympathy, "Yes, I understand you are a very busy man, maybe you know someone less busy who needs some work. I don't want to make problems for you; any person will be fine for my painting." I turned to his friend in the leather jacket, "Maybe you, you do not seem so busy."

Mr. Leather jacket's eyes bulged and they consulted each other in Arabic quickly and as indecipherably as before. With a show of nonchalance I turned to look down the alley, as though I were considering nearby people as possible models. "Tourists I allow to take photos sometimes of me and always I charge, but you are like a sister to me. I am happy to do this for you. My pleasure," Isham said smiling and bowing slightly. Then his eyes became serious, "250 dirham."

In the end I talked him down to 150 dirham for two hours and we agreed to meet the next afternoon. I was a little unhappy with the price but with him came a colorful store we could sit in front of in a relatively quiet, clean alley. He was tall and thin, younger than I was and clean shaven. He wore a worn white djellaba and a dark tie-dyed scarf wrapped around his head. I could already envision a painting where he was framed by a background of hanging rugs. I decided I would call the painting, "The Rug Salesman of Essaouira" or perhaps just, "Ali Baba."

I returned to my hotel and began a painting of the late afternoon sun through the curtains of my window. The open window shutters were a dark blue and the deep colors of the sunset blasted past their edges and washed out the white buildings on the street, making them translucent as ghosts.

* * *

The softest, smokiest part of dawn filtered in through my window. I lay on my side and studied the wrinkled expanse of sheet sprawling empty and barren next to me. It was early; I could feel the hour without even checking my watch. My painting bag lay packed and ready, needing only to be lifted and swung to my shoulder but I didn't move. I simply lay, studied the sheet and allowed myself to feel the silence of the room, filled only by the sound of my breathing.

When I got up to eat breakfast it was leftovers of dry, stale bread with a wedge of overpriced cheese that I nibbled from the edge of my bed as I watched the street below begin to stir and rustle itself awake. I finally left the room but detoured to the hotel café for mint tea and time to read and think. I had traded my addiction to the thick powerful Turkish coffee which gave energy but left me weak and shaking hours later, for the aphrodisiac qualities of the Moroccan mint tea. The tea was a drug both relaxing and simultaneously electrifying.

As I sipped my tea I knew it was uncertainty which held me back. It was time to begin a new painting but I was unsure of my next subject. Almost an hour later, without thinking I found myself rising, paying for breakfast, and then making my way to the fishing docks. There was an early morning haze which hung over the coast, at times remaining all day in spite of wind and sun. It was not quite a fog but it leeched the color from distant buildings and gave the medina walls, which soared above ocean battered rocks, a dreamy fairytale quality. The sea that morning was a churning frothy brown that hurled itself against the shore. What had been a gentle breeze by my hotel became a malicious gusting wind on the open walkways by the docks and I could feel the weight of it shoving at me like a hand.

I stood for a moment and tried to argue myself out of the location but the slanting morning sun enchanted the distant stone walls and stroked the long blue planks of the little wood fishing boats. Near me the fish market was opening up, fishermen called back and forth to each other, and long trays of fresh catch were being laid out. As I set up in the limited shade of the Skala du Port gate, I knew the sun would soon move and be in my eyes, glaring off my canvas. The wind rocked me on my feet though there was a wall to my back and just imagining the havoc it would wreak with my easel made me wince. In the end I found I did not care, I had to make the attempt. What sort of an artist would I be if I allowed every little inconvenience to deter me?

I thought of the impressionists, my favorites, like the Spanish painter Sorolla. Joaquin Sorolla would take his entire family to the coast; setting up a large canvas right on the sand with a tent erected above, to keep the sun off of his head. Then he would paint his children swimming in the surf. What had attracted my eye to his paintings was not the great detail; it was the looseness, the broad strokes, the light, the color, the sense of movement. He went for the big shapes because nature forced him to improvise, and compose quickly. There was no time to make a safe dozen pools of premixed paint but instead, in the beginning, only a few central mixes which could be added to as the painting progressed.

My left hand held my easel to keep the wind from flipping the whole apparatus over while the right whizzed across the canvas, condensing highlights to large passages, abstract shapes. When I was unsure of the color I aimed instead for the correct tone, and put in a neutral. I narrowed my eyes against the heavy wind and blurred my sight until all shapes vanished, looking for the brightest tone and then the darkest. Quickly I laid in those two key values which would be used later as reference points by which the other tones could be compared.

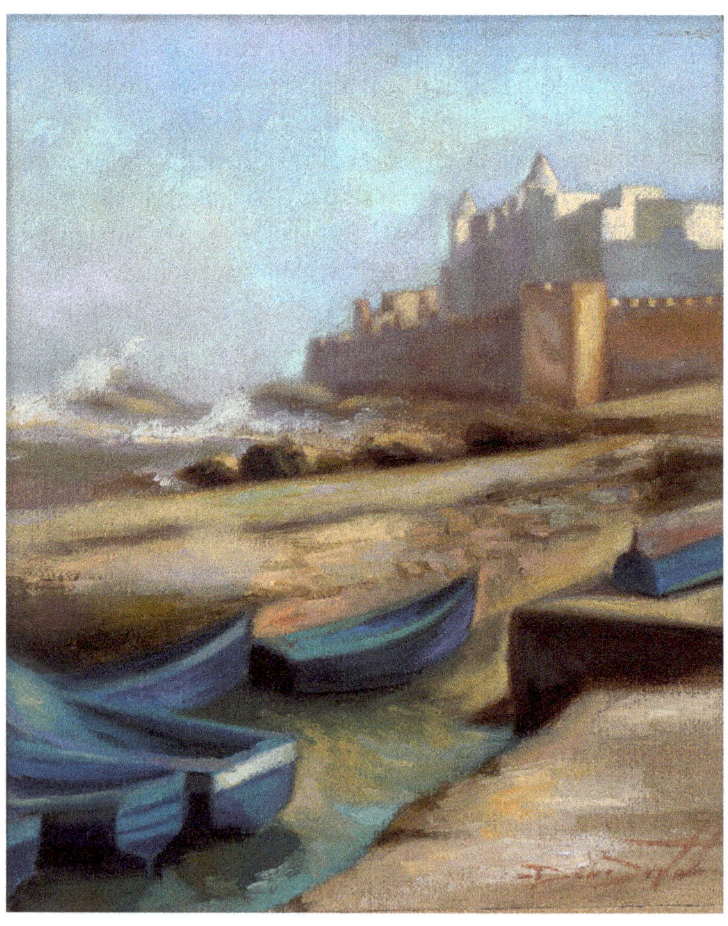

There was a time as a student when I studied and studied the looseness of some of the more famous impressionistic outdoor paintings. Van Gogh's screaming colors in the south of France especially intrigued me. His almost frantic, pulsating brushstrokes, I could not begin to duplicate. I knew now it was because I had been working too slowly. I had all the time in the world in my small studio. It was quiet and clean, my favorite music played soothingly. How could I paint the wildness of the wind, the chaos of the waves smashing against the rocks unless that same wind buffeted me and I was not separate from the landscape but a part of it? I thought of Van Gogh standing outside somewhere in a field in Arles, sweating, dehydrated, the sun beating down on him and the jaded, wicked mistral grabbing at his canvas and upending his brushes. He had probably been tired, nearly delirious, sweat running into his eyes, blurring the edges of his vision, his hands may have even trembled a little but he had been determined to capture the feel of that hot sun eating into him. He wrote to his brother Theo while living and painting in Arles:

"Today again, from seven o'clock in the morning till six in the evening, I worked without stirring except to eat a bite a step or two away. That is why the work is getting on fast. But what will you say to it? And what shall I think of it myself a little while from now? I have a lover's clear sight or a lover's blindness.

These colours give me extraordinary exaltation. I have no thought of fatigue; I shall do another picture this very night, and I shall bring it off. I have a terrible lucidity at moments when nature is so beautiful; I am not conscious of myself anymore, and the pictures come to me as in a dream." –Vincent Van Gogh, Dear Theo

Above my head, the seagulls screamed and swooped, I was in danger of being showered with bird poop. The tourists stared and tried to wedge close enough to see my progress and the wind rocked my tripod viciously. All detail work became impossible. Still, I had a solid sketch well started when I finally packed up. The morning light had changed enough that shadow shapes were growing smaller and changing tone, plus I needed to grab some lunch before I met up with Isham.

I was pretty proud of arranging the modeling session. The person I used to be would have gone straight to my hotel room to paint the late setting sun rather than searching down the alley for a model. Later of course, I had sat in my room second guessing myself, full of doubts about the price we had agreed on, and whether or not I would be able to get enough out of the painting to justify the time and extra expense. Thinking of it as I stood in the wind, paint smeared on my fingers, my hair a snarled mass tangled about my face, struggling with my pack, I was amazed I had ever let myself doubt. The exhilaration of painting was worth any cost. I felt as I painted the local people, the buildings, the light, even in a way to imply the smells, the sounds that I had come to a better understanding and appreciation of my surroundings. Painting made me feel more sure of who I was, whereas without my canvas my life narrowed with lack of meaning. The act of creating filled me with a great love and compassion for everything around me.

As I walked down the alley to Isham's store, my paints prepped, a fresh canvas in hand I could see Isham was there, waiting for me. He wore the long white robe of the desert people and the same black tie-dyed cloth wrapped carelessly around his head. I was greeted with a smile and as I set down my pack and considered the alleyway he went and borrowed a couple of stools.

I set up across from his shop, the front of which was hung with handmade rugs which continued down the length of the alley, patches of color which warmed the surrounding stone. He sat across from me, watching as I opened my paint box and fixed my canvas to the lid. Finally I sat back and simply looked at him. I didn't want to pose him, I wanted him relaxed and natural, or as natural as anyone could appear who had a stranger sitting and staring at them for hours. I decided not to have him face me; I wasn't prepared to weather his gaze. At all times I felt myself an observer drinking in the details of life but I disliked being observed. I coveted invisibility and while I longed for the challenge and intensity of my model staring straight out of the canvas, I wasn't ready. As he turned his head so he faced off to the side, his eyes were cast in velvet shadow and the cobalt blue rug behind him seemed to absorb him, as though he were part of its subtle pattern.

Once I began to paint he barely moved and seemed to hardly need breaks even to stretch. As I painted he told me that his family lived near Merzoga at the edge of the Sahara and they were Tourag Berbers, nomads. His face had a mix of black and Arab features, thin and finely boned with high cheekbones, a strong brow, and elegant nose. His black head wrap which had intermittent streaks of yellow, purple, and red served to make his features even more prominent in the soft light of the alley.

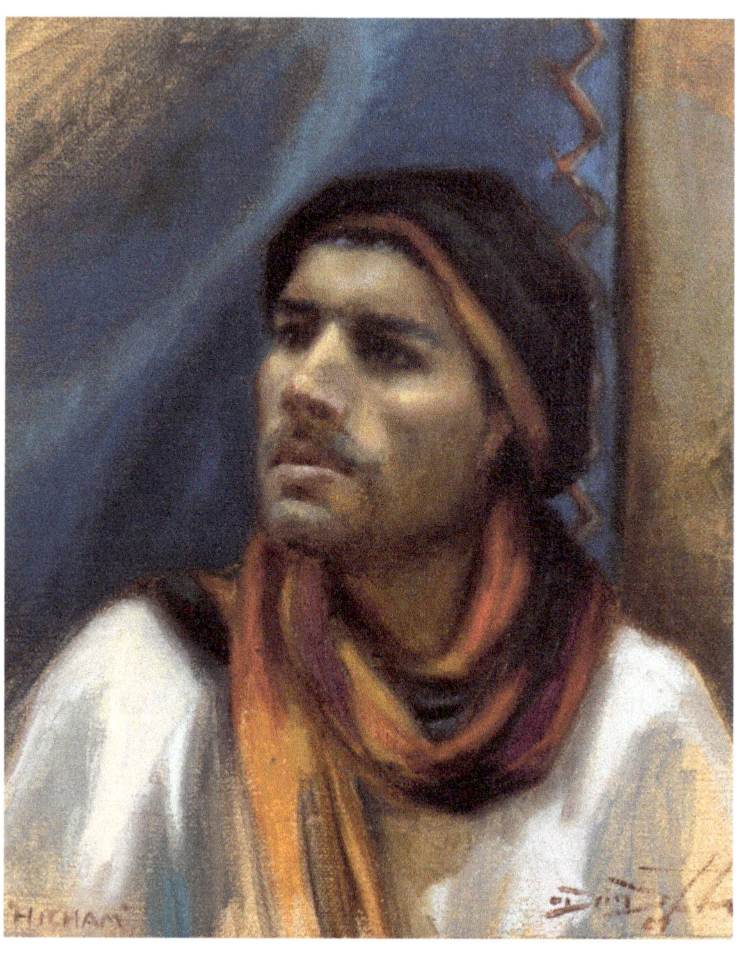

Boys were playing soccer nearby and several times the ball slammed into the wall next to my arm. Each time, without moving Isham would snap briskly in Arabic and the little boys would sigh and move their game a little farther off, only to gradually make their way closer minutes later. It was as though even as they were absorbed in their game, they were pulled by an invisible well of gravity, and Isham and I were the center of a cosmic black hole.

He looked at the painting only when it was finished and then was silent as he studied his own features with greater attention to detail than he probably gave the reflection that faced him daily in the mirror. The painting was not a photograph; it was not faithful in cold precision. It was his face strained through the silk filter of my mind, as though a leaving of gold dust after the silt of the river had been shaken free. It was a biased reproduction, flawed with small distortions and in the end more of a feeling than an image. It was the heat of the desert, it was firelight under the stars, it was silence in a hall of sand dunes.

"You have done me great honor," he said at last. "Of anyone you chose to paint, you chose me and you have taken great care." He nodded as he began to hand the painting back. "You are like a sister to me. I could tell from the beginning, you are a nice girl. You do not need to pay me. It has been a great honor."

"No, please," I said embarrassed. "I am paying you for your time. I know how boring it is for you to sit there and you did such a good job." I looked down at the wet painting, and it seemed so much stronger than the two I had done in Taroudannt. It had been easier and faster to paint as well. It had all seemed to flow out of the brush as though it had already existed but had just been waiting to be born. "Do you know any women who might like to model?"

Isham frowned and thought, "This is difficult, many women cover their faces and they are busy in the home. Or their husbands would not like this so much... but I know one woman maybe. It is no problem that she is old and not so beautiful?"

"No, no of course not, anyone would be fine; I just want some local people to sit for me, both men and women."

"I will see her tonight. I will ask, then tomorrow, insha'allah."

* * *

I got out of bed the next morning nearly before I had opened my eyes, quicker than thought in one single fluid, decisive motion. Down at the docks I found the gusting wind of the day before had been replaced by a faint lively breeze which made conditions perfect to work on my shore sketch. After a couple hours of rechecking the drawing and pushing the sunlight effect on the buildings brighter, the wind began to pick up again and tired, I returned to my hotel. By 1pm I had refreshed my paints, grabbed a new canvas and was on my way to meet up with Isham and see if he had good news for me.

When I arrived at the alley he wasn't there but the artist from a few days before was and I decided to go back into his gallery to see his work. I stood in a back room before a wall of paintings wondering how long I needed to spend looking, how much time was required for courtesy. I was trying to look interested and thoughtful when he poked his head into the room.

"Are you still looking for a female model?"

I turned, "yes, yes of course."

"One of the salesmen in the gallery knows a woman who could model for you. He does not speak very much English though and the woman does not speak any at all."

"That's okay, I am sure we could make do. When could she sit for me?"

He turned and called out and a man appeared at his shoulder. He had a soft open face, the line of his mouth was full and vulnerable and there was an air about him of one who was easily surprised and often teased. They had a brief conversation before they turned back to me. "When would you like to paint her? You are free now?"

"Yes, I was waiting to see if Isham would show up because he thought he might know somebody but I can always come back later. If she is free now, that would be great, but if not, later is fine too."

They spoke quickly, a slurring rush of consonants and vowels, like the cadences of a song. "Now is good, he will take you to the home." I was waved out the door and as I began to follow the unknown man, a stranger, I realized I could not even ask him how far it was. Would we leave the walls of the old city? Did we have to take a car? Who was this woman that he knew and how did he know whether or not she would be free without notice?

He led me through a maze of small connecting alleys, footpaths at one turn smelling of spices and sawdust, and at another the sweet reek of sewage, the mustiness of standing water. We didn't leave the city walls but I had lost track of where we were by the time he stopped at a door and gesturing for me to wait, unlocked it and bounded up a flight of stairs. I stood and wondered if it was a good idea. Who knew where I was? Only the man at the gallery. What if this was an elaborate setup to get me alone? How well could I trust any of these people? My paint box, the canvas held tightly in my hands, the tripod under my arm, they kept me from turning and leaving, they rooted my feet like anchors. As long as I had them I knew who I was and I was willing to take some chances, to have a little faith.

He emerged after five minutes and beckoned me to follow him. The stairway branched off to closed doors on each landing, little apartments I realized as he led me through one. We stood in a small entryway with a tall ceiling, placed high on the wall was a single window, which was the apartment's only source of natural light. A small doorway directly in front of us led to a closet-sized kitchen and an arching doorway immediately to my left opened onto a large room lined on two sides with a cushioned blue bench sofa, while underfoot the floor was layered with woven mats and rugs. At one end a TV sat with a smug air and at the other end a curtain closed off a small alcove which contained a double bed and wardrobe.

A small one year old boy galloped to meet us, his excitement so immense he careened off our knees in a scramble and was vaulting off another corner of the room like an aberrant ping pong ball before I could take a breath. A woman stood to greet me, a slight flush on her high cheekbones, her dark eyes sparkling like wet stones. Her youth was in its highest most radiant bloom. I felt foolish as I realized that of course, he had brought me home to paint his wife. It was not I who had been taking a chance on him but he, who was taking a chance on me, allowing a stranger into his refuge. I felt a tug on the easel in my hand and realized his son was gnawing on the end of it. With a cluck his wife scooped him up and began to nurse him in the corner.

I frowned at the single light source. The sitting area was completely dark except for the space directly around the doorway and the vestibule itself was too cramped to set up in. I could achieve light on my model but would have very little on my canvas and palette. I gave a little inward sigh as I set up as near to the door as I could get. As I pulled out my brushes I hesitated, wondering where I could put them so they would be out of reach of the baby but within reach of me. Glancing over at his wife I realized she had cleverly done the one thing possible to ensure peace for the two of us. Finished nursing, the little boy had fallen asleep and moving with great care she carried him to the bed.

Her husband knew my preference for traditional clothes and they ransacked the wardrobe in an effort to find something. A black scarf was produced and speedily wrapped about her head and lower face. Lacking traditional robes, a plaid orange blanket was rustled up which his wife belted in place with a filmy pink scarf, submerging herself in heavy folds like a delicate fleshed sea creature burying itself in sand. I eyed the concoction with skepticism. She was completely mummified, her hands had vanished, the wide sensual mouth, even the sweep of fine boned nose had disappeared.

Mentally I flashed back to early that morning when walking through the market I had passed a group of robed women, one with only a fraction of an inch of skin showing around her eyes which were covered by sunglasses. Just fifteen minutes before I had seen this woman's bare breast as she nursed their child, now I was standing in front of a woman so encased in blanket that anything resembling the shape of a person beneath was gone. I felt overheated just looking at her. She couldn't possibly be comfortable, I decided. How she could breathe was beyond me. With a gesture at my face and a shrug I tried to communicate to her husband that I missed her face and perhaps this was maybe a little too traditional. I could tell by his eyes he understood what I wanted and his expression was cool as he shook his head. With a sweep of his hand to his wife, he let me know that the only way she would sit for me was if she were completely covered.

I shrugged and smiled as I finished with my last preparations and with a few gestures had waved her into the corner where I wanted her to sit. After her husband left to go back to work I realized how incredibly fortunate I was to be female. If I had been a traveling male painter I would not have been allowed alone with his wife. Even had I been allowed to paint a man's wife he would have insisted on staying to chaperone and I would have had to pay double for the privilege.

She settled herself in a corner on a pile of cushions where the light from the window would fall on her and as I looked at her I faced a definite portrait challenge. Her eyes were intoxicating.

She had exotic thin arching brows and the black liquid pools of her eyes were softened and enveloped by violet shadows. There was only the briefest glimpse of the upper portion of her cheek bones and a small triangle of glowing forehead visible. Yet, by covering everything else, the eyes seemed magnified in importance, as if to hint at all that was covered. That small glimpse of skin teased at the unseen shape of lips and chin. Her eyes had to carry her entire personality. They had to hint at laughter and sorrow, black tangled cobweb of scented hair, secretive sensual smiles, the mystique of the feminine, a sway of hips, an arching wrist, a turn of ankle.

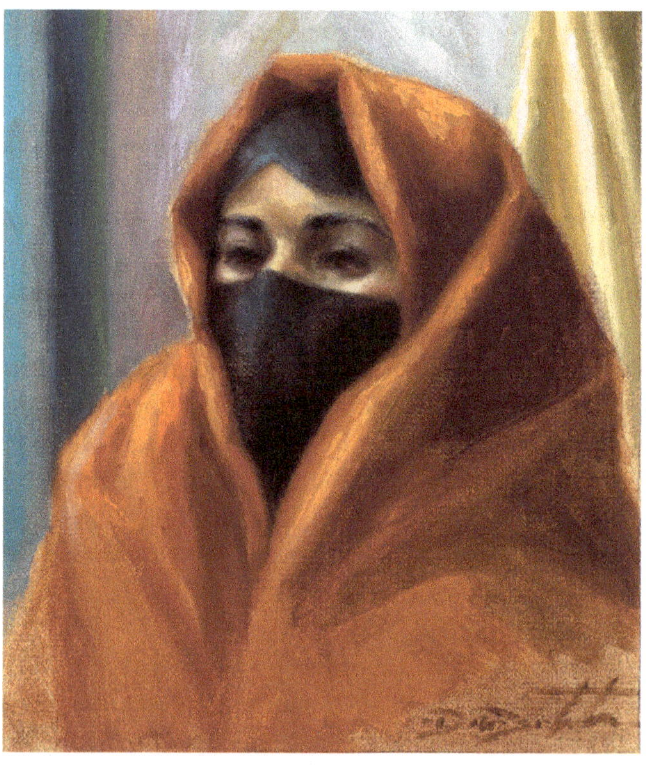

I found it interesting that one minute this woman was cleaning her home, taking care of her child, it was just another regular day with its rhythms and routines. Then unexpectedly her husband had arrived home and at his command she was to put her whole day on hold without question or complaint. She had to swath herself in unbelievable stuffy layers to sit still as a statue for a total stranger to paint.

The feminists of my country would have called it oppression, subjugation, implemented by a lack of education and opportunities. Yet, she did not seem an unhappy woman. In Morocco it seemed to me what society valued for women was a good marriage to a stable provider, a home, a son, and she had all of those things. After all, posing for a foreigner had to be a novelty of sorts, a new exotic event to break up the tedium of repetitive tasks.

In many ways Morocco was a very modern country in comparison to many Muslim countries and the roles of women were constantly changing. In 2002 Mudawanna was put into place protecting women's rights to divorce and custody. Women were allowed to choose whether they wore the veil, though they were still strongly influenced by their family. More unmarried women went uncovered then married women who preferred to conceal themselves in public. It was a different culture and a different value system. My life was so dissimilar. My priorities and desires would be incomprehensible to her, just as hers flit past and through me. At the same time, the lack of a common language swept aside verbal communication, politics, religion, women's rights. All of it fell away until what was left was only the two of us, model and artist, in an oasis of peace. For just a small feather of time, we were bound together.

While their son slept I worked quickly, ever aware that as soon as he woke up she would be forced to move to care for him. Then the folds of her makeshift robe would shift and change and because a good portion of the painting was that all-encompassing, hideous, orange blanket, it had to be put in correctly. While the blanket could be mapped in quickly with a large brush to unite folds, the area around the eyes was far more of a challenge. A woman's features were more delicate then a man's so the brush strokes had to correspond in delicacy and because all that could be seen were her eyes it was highly important that their proportions and symmetry, as well as tone and shading were perfect. It could be a painting of a shapeless mound with two eyes squinting out or it could be a subtle, seductive painting that hinted at more than it revealed. The woman beneath the robe was a mystery. Her hopes, fears, character would normally be revealed in the curve of the mouth; age hinted at in the lines of the face, all of it was denied the viewer. She could be everyone and no one. She represented all women, all faces, all longings, all desires.

After only an hour and a half there was a loud knock at the door. My model's eyes widened as she stared at me and we both held our breath, listening. There was a rustle from the alcove, a murmur, and then a low, slowly building wail. The baby had woken and even as she rose and rushed to him I had a feeling that none of her efforts would get him back to sleep. Some minutes later she returned chagrined and even as she took her spot, he emerged red faced and grumpy, annoyed at not having her attention. Keeping one eye on my loose brushes and palette knife, ready to rescue them should he approach I finished as quickly as I was able. She seemed relieved when I motioned she could get up and care for him. I needed only to work on the background a little more, pushing the effect of the glow of the wall behind her head.

She began to shed layers as though casting off filmy translucent veils, abandoning the husk of a chrysalis and rising, stretching. I glanced up at her and wondered if I had managed to capture any part of her. She glanced at me then away quickly, suddenly shy and disappeared to clatter invisible dishes in her kitchen. She reappeared with a glass of fresh squeezed orange juice and a bowl of fresh dates and figs, determined to show me hospitality. Adrian had told me before he left that to eat or drink during the day in front of a Muslim who was observing the holy fasting month of Ramadan was the height of rudeness. At the same time I could tell by her insistence that to turn down her refreshments would be far ruder, as though what she had to offer was not good enough. It was difficult because she only spoke Arabic, so I laughed and told her all the Arabic words I knew which combined covered only the most basic of pleasantries.

A few last touches and I sat back, finished with the sketch. I needed to see the painting in better light but what I could accomplish at the moment was complete. I looked up at her and handed the painting over. Looking at it she blushed and laughed, covering her face with her hands as though embarrassed. Returning to it after a minute she tilted her head as she considered then pointed out the one aspect of the painting not true to life, I had left out the plaid pattern on the orange blanket. I rolled my eyes and shrugged, artist's prerogative. I had decided that little detail did not particularly add to the sketch in any kind of significant way and did not feel I had the time to really work it in with any great success. As I rose to leave she ran to her wardrobe and rattling through a few drawers came quickly back to put into my hands a traditional Tourag beaded necklace. I wanted to beat my head against the wall because I didn't have anything on me to give her in return, as a keepsake.

After a few wrong turns I managed to find my way back to my hotel and once there reworked a few parts of the sketch while the paint was still wet. Leaning the painting board against the wall then sitting back from it across the room, the little colorful rectangle seemed like a window. The Moroccan woman sat shrouded in orange folds, her thoughts hidden, yet there was a softness to her, such a sense of yielding about her eyes. Behind her a twist of yellow cloth broke the grayish blue of the wall and the hour of the day was masked by the vague indirect light. It was as though she had sat motionless for a very long time, so long that time had ceased to exist and somewhere she still sat, waiting for the day to end. It was not my strongest sketch. I felt that perhaps my painting of Isham was more successful, yet there was a feeling to the painting which was more than I could have hoped for.

* * *

The buildings were leached of color and their outlines had been lost in the quality of a half dream, the moment between waking and sleeping, only a memory of reality to give them substance. I stood in front of my window and stared out at early morning fog which would make working on the sky portion of my port painting quite difficult. My choices were to go down, drink tea and read until the fog lifted or attempt a new painting of the ramparts of the port gate blurred and lost, an effect which could change at any time.

With a sigh I picked up my paint bag and taped a fresh canvas to my board. I walked to the port quickly, holding my breath, in a silent changed world, murky in half light. I set up and mixed my paint mixtures in record time, but still I was only forty-five minutes into the sketch before the fog lifted leaving me blinking in the sun and assaulted by flies. I trudged back to the hotel and retrieved the first port painting, brought it back, and finished it. I wasn't sure how I felt about it when I was done. My mind was still locked into the fog, that still, timeless haze, that sense of being the last person on earth, as though everything and everyone around me had been momentarily misplaced.

I walked through the streets of the town for awhile afterward. I left a message for Isham with one of his friends, that if he would like to model I would be by the next day at 3pm. Next I went to the gallery and gave the salesman a necklace I had bought some years ago in Germany to give to his wife and told him to look among his family members and find me someone I could paint the next day. He seemed dazed and amused by me but I hoped he understood and I crossed my fingers as I left that when I returned one or the other of the two model prospects would be available.

I found myself a little later standing in front of a bank of phones, the sun warm on my shoulders and the gulls wheeling above crying out over and over as though lost. I gripped the plastic tightly in my hand and listened to the tiny electronic sound of ringing on the other end, on and on, such a small hopeless sort of noise.

"Yeah...hello?" his voice was rough with sleep and an image of warm tangled sheets rose in my mind as real as the sun on my back and the breeze running through my hair.

"Isn't it a little late for you to still be sleeping?

"Hey...mmmm just a nap, I was watching a movie and I fell asleep." The phone line went quiet and I wondered if he could hear the cry of the birds behind me, if he was visualizing me standing dwarfed by the ancient city walls, even as I was picturing him, face lit by the flicker of a silent TV screen, sleep softening his features, the memory of dreams dusting his skin. My heart hurt as the silence spun out, I listened to the digital click of money disappearing and I wondered why we had nothing to say.

"So...have you been busy?" I asked.

He sighed, "training, you know just getting ready. How are you? How is painting?"

I closed my eyes and concentrated on breathing, feeling suddenly disappointed. How separate we were, his life was completely focused on how to become a better soldier, a better lethal instrument for the government, whereas my every thought was toward trying to capture the unseen essence of life, that glowing elusive flicker of something so intangible, so precious, so brief. I tried to hold onto the memory of the sound of our laughter together in my mind, the heat of his presence and I felt very alone, very alone and very far away. "Fine," I said, "Everything is going fine."

"Good, glad to hear it babe. Look, this is probably costing you a lot and I'm sorry I just woke up and..."

"Yeah, I know, I just wanted to hear your voice,"

"Well it was good hearing yours, I miss you. You know that, right?"

I sighed and nodded, knowing he couldn't see the movement. Even after he hung up I held the phone in my hand, listening to the silence on the other end, wishing there were words, words that were saying what I needed to hear.

* * *

As soon as I woke the next morning I flew to my window hoping blindly and was relieved when I saw fog. It was the earliest I had yet risen and when I emerged into the lobby I found the room pitch black and the front door locked. The hotel was heavy with sleep and silence as I groped along the wall for a light switch but turned up nothing. I ran my fingers along the chalky surface of the wall until I reached the large, ironbound front door. Running my hands over the locking mechanism, I prayed it was only bolted, not secured with a key. I bent my face down trying to see anything. The darkness had almost the feel of a space underground, devouring, as though it had a gravity well which absorbed and annihilated light. Finally I found the catch. With a click, the door swung open and I allowed myself to breathe again as I eased outside.

When I got to my painting spot the fog was so thick that not only were all walls lost, the rocks and ocean had vanished as well into a serpentine undulating mist that seemed nearly alive. In the painting I had begun the day before, the soft shrouded outline of the Skala du Port had been visible against a grey opaque sky, with the sun just barely starting to burn through. I began to mix my paints, creating large pools based on my mixtures of the day before and new tones that I could observe before me. I worked a little on the sky portion, which was one effect that had remained consistent but beyond that I was waiting. I felt a little like a cat staring down a mouse hole, tense, expectant, nerve endings wired and ready. When the fog began to lift, it would lift fast and I had to be ready for it.

Painting in the fog was a new experience in many ways, things sounded differently, cats and seagulls sat almost next to each other on the walkway, watching and waiting. It was as though everything was holding its breath. One of the seagulls kept crying in an uncertain way that sounded exactly like the meowing of a nervous cat or at times deep and low enough to be the muffled, groaning low of a cow. The world seemed frozen and beneath the stillness lay a latent energy that not only thrilled through my own nerves but seemed echoed in the flagstones and silent buildings. It was as though everything waited only for the curtain to be raised before shaking off the spell and waking up.

Finally, an hour later the sun began to burn through casting a faint gold glow on the medieval looking walls and jagged outlines of the ocean rocks. My brush flew and I was finished half an hour later as around me shops opened doors and pails of water were thrown onto walkways, washing the memory of the night from the pavement. There was no trace of fog as the gulls lifted themselves into the morning air, circling above the moored fishing boats in the hopes of scraps and the cats stretched before submerging themselves in shadows.

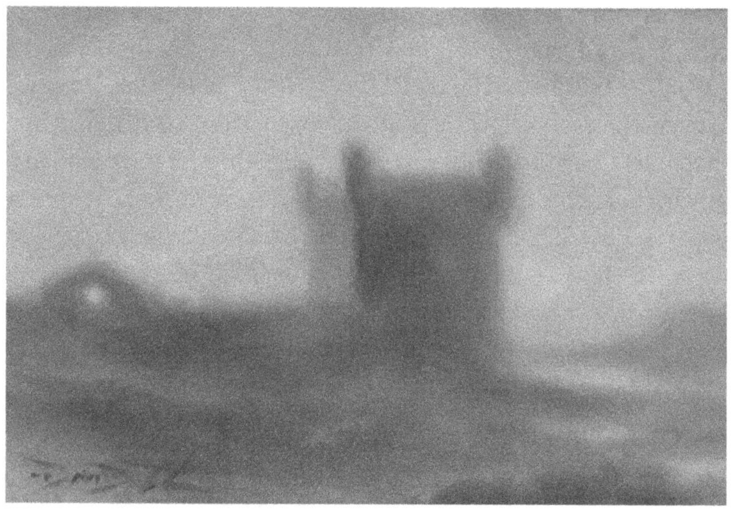

As I walked back to my hotel I studied the result, a small, vague, smudgy sketch, that in the bright sunlight seemed unreal, imagined, created, not observed. After breakfast I got out a fresh canvas and made my way to a new painting site.

Inside the battlements of the Skala du Port was a roughly-cut stone room bordered on one side by a stone archway and on the other by massive, half open, wooden doors which led outside. High above, a small stone window pierced through the thick walls to let in glowing light that sifted over the discolored rock of the walls, creating a very clean, uncluttered effect, different from the busy, detailed atmosphere of the shop alleys.

In a few hours I managed to cover the canvas, mapping the composition out with a thin layer of paint and turpentine before going back to my room, getting a fresh canvas and prepping my paint for a model.

I went back to my now very familiar alley and found Isham who confirmed that in two hours he would pose for me. He seemed very pleased and amused that I had returned to hire him again, he could not stop shaking his head and laughing. Then I went to the gallery and found my guide of the day before and asked if he had found any more family to pose for me. He looked surprised and alarmed and after making sure a male model would be fine he offered his services and went off to procure a head wrap. He was back only minutes later and one of the other salesmen helped him put it on rolling his eyes at me and telling me he should charge him a 100 dirham for the service because now he would have to work while my model would be paid to sit on his butt and do nothing. We all laughed and I was made comfortable on a padded stool in their courtyard while my new model sat in front of an elaborately carved antique door. He wore a bright red head wrap that brought out the reds in his ruddy cheeks. He was lighter complexioned then the others, more Arab and European in coloring, with a round, young, unlined face, a thin moustache, and a full rosebud like mouth that remained slightly open as he sat with a bewildered almost doe-like air about him.

The others were alternately amused at his expense, then at mine but after very little commotion settled back into their respective places. The man in the armchair next to him read his paper for awhile before folding it over his face and falling asleep. My artist friend, who it turned out ran the large gallery which was owned by his family, came after only half an hour to check on my progress. I only had a bare minimum laid on in paint and I laughed as he looked over my shoulder. "It doesn't look like anything yet." I said, "It's too soon, you have to check again later."

"Oh no... it definitely looks like something, but not him. I have known him a long time." With a nod he left again and I settled into my chair and let the quiet of the afternoon seep into me.

The atmosphere of the gallery was different from that of my model's apartment the day before. I felt a languorous lassitude, as though the day belonged to me and nothing would occur to interrupt the tranquility. Very few tourists emerged through the door, and those who did were given a few minutes to roam before being greeted by one of the other salesmen. There was none of the scrambling and aggressive sales talk that occurred in the bazaars of Marrakesh or Fez. They explained to me later that their gallery was listed in several guidebooks and most people who found them eventually bought something. The art of the sale was soft and subtle, I scarcely noticed any of it as my model sat facing me, seeming nearly transfixed, as though afraid to even breathe.

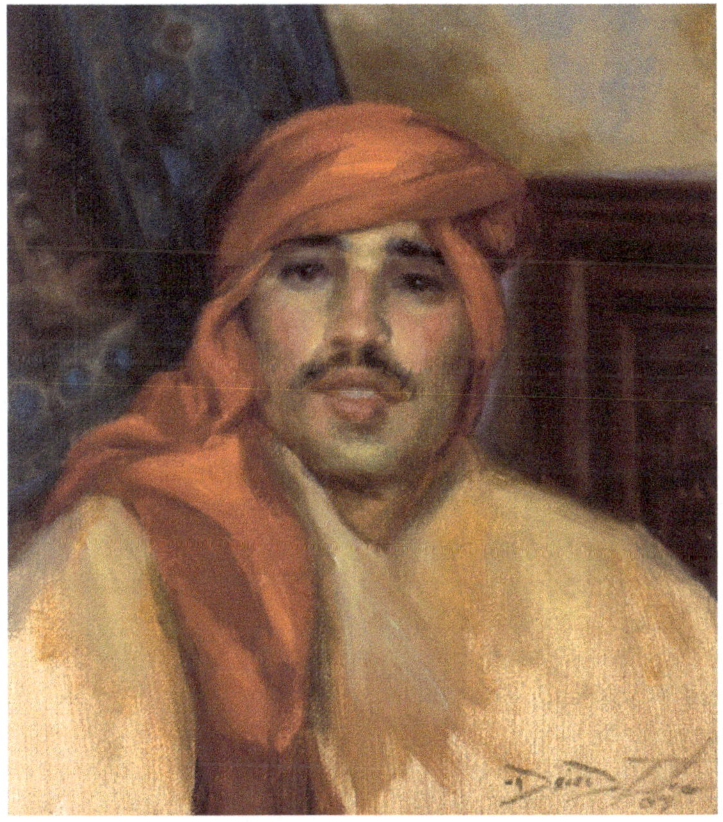

It flowed; painting him seemed as simple as casting myself into a pool of still, salt water where only a bare flicker of movement was needed to remain afloat. There was no concern, no conflict, one moment the canvas held a collection of shapes, tones, flowing into light rhythms, coalescing into patterns, and then it became him, mouth parted with that delicious sense of the unknown, the unfamiliar. Head slightly tilted, the red cloth falling around his head to drape down one shoulder, and eyes alive, full, and rich. For once it was effortless.

By the time I finished with my model two hours later, the artist had returned and stood behind me silently saying nothing. I said with a nervous laugh, "So, it still does not look like him?"

He looked at me and shook his head slowly, "No... No, it is him, exactly."

"Oh," I sighed with pleasure. "Thank you. May I return tomorrow to finish painting the wood door behind him into the background?"

"You may return as often as you like, you are welcome here." He nodded and disappeared deeper into the gallery as I began to pack up. I went outside and found Isham who looked a little distracted. Apparently he had been very sick the day before but was much better. Still we decided to postpone his session until the next day at 3pm.

I started to walk down to the wood working shops to check on my frames and part of the way there I was hailed, "Hey painter! Hey artist!"I turned around and saw a young Moroccan man who had been trying for days to get my attention as I walked past and curious at his persistence I decided to see what he wanted.

"Artist, you paint me, I am Berber." I tilted my head and considered him. At first glance he was a light skinned black man with a goatee and a gap toothed smile. He was not handsome but he had a quality far more attractive and elusive, he was interesting. He had the luminescence of burning ambitious youth in his large, clear, intelligent eyes which combined with a hint of street urchin reflected in his worn clothes. He was bold. There was something about him that reminded me of my father, the elusive gleam of fearless drive.

I nodded slowly, "Okay, how about the day after tomorrow? 10:30 in the morning."

"Yes madam, my name is Youssef. I will be here, there is my shop," he pointed past me down another alley hanging with rugs. "I am Berber madam. Berber, desert people."

"Okay, great, see you then." I smiled as I waved goodbye and continued on my way only to be accosted five minutes later.

"Hey, artist! Hey, painter!" I turned around, a skinny pale guy bounded up to me rattling on a bewildering spiel about the fine artwork in his shop. I had some time and with a shrug decided to follow him. As we passed my wood working shop I picked up my frames and we continued on with the guy prattling on about tours to the Sahara. When I got to his shop, I found Youssef to whom I had spoke not fifteen minutes earlier, I had been led there by his cousin who was also named Youssef. I started to laugh as I told my guide that I had been to his shop before and would be back in a few days. "Madam, you could paint me!" the new Youssef offered as he followed me out the door.

"No, no I am sorry, I am too busy the next few days, but maybe later on."

"Okay, maybe another day, but you come back. I am Youssef! Ask for Youssef!"

* * *

I had to unlock the front door of the hotel again the next morning to get out, though I had no pressing reason to be up so early. I decided to explore parts of the old city I had not seen before and walked around the city's outer wall until I reentered into an unfamiliar section. I wandered the back alleys looking for new painting subjects, peeking around corners at each small, badly lit footpath cast to dusk by the loom of buildings that pressed close on either side. Silent, dim, shuttered windows, like stopped mouths, scattered overhead and below the cobblestones seemed never to end.

Nothing gripped me, nothing tugged at my eyes and finally when I was stopped dead in my tracks it was not by a sight but by a smell. Faint then stronger, rising dough, a layer of sugar, whiff of honey, heating jam, flaking layers browning in the heat of an oven. I closed my eyes and breathed in; all that was missing was the smell of coffee. I slowly walked backwards until I found myself in front of a glass case filled with hot fresh pastries and a bemused woman who had paused in her sweeping to stare at me. I bought a bag of a variety of different kinds and she wrapped each one carefully in brown paper. I was in such a hurry to get to my room to devour them that I dropped the entire bag on my hotel stairwell and howled in frustration as they spilled out. I gritted my teeth, stuffed them back in the bag and once in my room ate them anyway.

I returned to the Skala du Port to finish the dim interior and stayed until the wind began to growl like a mad demon and blew so much sand and grit through the doorway that it coated my wet canvas and the paint mixtures on my palette. Up to that point there had been the added distraction of tour groups wandering through in bewildered huddles. A small half hidden stairwell to my back led up to the roof which had a panoramic 360 degree view. I became an impromptu tour guide pointing the stairwell out to every concerned tourist who could not find the rest of his party and without my assistance would walk back and forth in front of me sticking his or her head into adjoining rooms and terraces growing more and more baffled by the minute. The wind however finally proved stronger than my own determination, and with my eyes tearing and reddened from grit, I packed up.

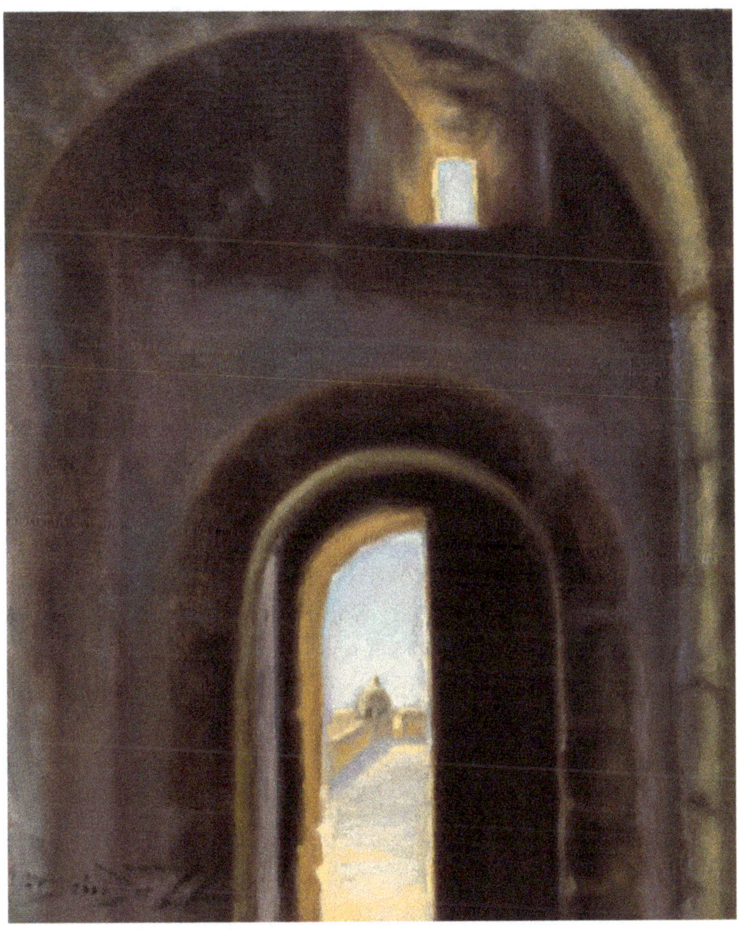

Hunched against the breeze I walked out and passed my old spot facing the walls of the city. There, by the crashing waves I saw two artists painting. They were an older, European looking couple with large canvases and expensive looking metal easels. I wanted to stop and watch, to speak to them, but remembering my own dislike of constant disruptions I paid them the best compliment in my arsenal and left them alone. Still my mind clamored with questions. Who were they? Where were they from? Here were two more people braving the elements, dive bombing seagulls attracted by the fish market, and the endless curiosity of passerby. I was no longer unique.

Back at the hotel I refined the Skala painting for another hour. The main problem with the location was that while there was perfect light hitting the subject there was not enough light on the canvas. What looked good in the murky twilight of the stone room became a disaster out in the light.

After I cleaned up my palette and brushes I headed to the gallery to work on the background behind the portrait I had begun the day before. It was a lazy day for them because even the owner sat and took a nap in one of the chairs. The haze of peace was intoxicating. I found myself lingering over the painting wishing to draw it out, not to finish, because finishing meant having to rise and break the utterly delicious tranquility. I only had an hour however, to work on the antique door before I needed to pack up to meet Isham.

He was waiting for me in front of his shop with a light blue scarf with dark blue ends that he bound his head with expertly. The lightness of the scarf made his skin seem darker and richer and as I sat slightly across and beneath him he raised his chin in a nearly arrogant gesture. He seemed then like a swarthy Lawrence of Arabia or noble sheikh staring out across the sands instead of a simple rug seller staring at a blank stone wall. He was however, less focused this time and it took all of my skill and patience to capture him because he would not stop moving or talking. He had mentioned something a day or so earlier about quitting smoking so that could have been it but I found myself enjoying his company less because he spent the whole time trying to persuade me to let him either take me on a tour to the mountains, or the Sahara, or to buy some of his rugs. After awhile I stopped responding, only continued painting. I liked him but all of my time and money had to go towards painting which I had explained many times to him before and I didn't know how to make him understand. He finally became quiet toward the end when one of his friends said something that made him angry and he set his face and looked quite ferocious.

I sighed a little to myself as a shadow crossed onto my canvas then stayed. I finally looked up to see who was blocking my light. "Hi, do you speak English?"

I blinked in surprise at the tourist who was staring down at me. I was wearing a long sleeved shirt and pants, definitely not the sort of clothing a local woman would wear but then I was fairly dark. "Yeah, actually I am."

"No kidding, and you just... you know this guy or...?"

"I hire the locals to model for me. This is Isham, he owns this rug shop."

"I am an artist too, mostly I just take photographs that I use in my studio back home in London to paint and draw from. I just never thought it would really work, bringing all my supplies to a foreign country. I mean, just sitting out here on the street like this. You are so brave, doesn't anyone ever bother you? I mean my studio...I can't imagine working outside of it..."

I looked down at my painting, then across at Isham who was frowning in an effort to follow our conversation. "It can definitely be a challenge, trying to paint this way, I struggle with it but..." I shrugged, "I wouldn't have it any other way. You learn a lot from communicating with the locals, being in a place for hours at a time. I saw two other artists out by the port this morning painting, so I am not the only one but I didn't get a chance to talk to them or anything. I don't know what their story is."

"I don't know... I don't think I could do it. But hey, good luck."

"You too," I said as he turned to go.

I had to admit to myself it was intimidating to set up out of the controlled environment of the studio where there was a nearby supply of food and water, a toilet, predictable light, a closed door for privacy and best yet, no judgments or questions. But where was the fear and the excitement? The uncertainty? To arrive in town one day, with no idea what you would paint and the next day to be consumed by the latest inspiration. To me taking chances, living outside of my comfort zone, gave life more color and vibrancy and a fresher edge to my art.

I smiled reassuringly at Isham as I put in the finishing touches, pushing the light a little farther on the top of his turban, a glowing purple highlight on his forehead. The man in the sketch looked stoically off into the distance, nearly classically beautiful, the dark shadowed planes of his face, the far-off hooded gaze. Isham was not a beautiful man on first meeting but when he sat to pose some part of him changed. His face fell into poetic lines, until there was a near lovely melancholy, a sort of ageless romance about his face.

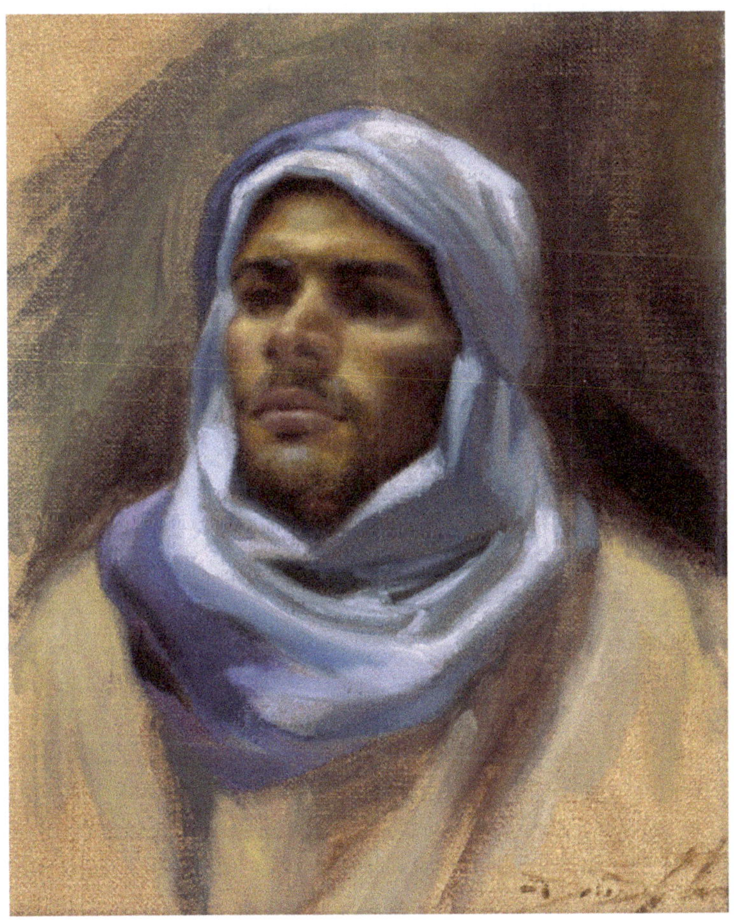

As a man approached, Isham eased out of his pose and into conversation gesturing at my sketch until the other man approached and looked over my shoulder. "This is my uncle," Isham said after a moment.

I looked up and smiled, "As-Salaam aleikum."

"Wa aleikum as- salaam," the other man murmured. He turned to Isham and spoke for a few minutes in Arabic before nodding at me and leaving.

"He says you can come to his house tomorrow afternoon and paint my aunt if you would like. After you finish at sundown you can eat with us."

I grinned, "Really? Isham that would be great!" He smiled and the tension of earlier seeped from his face.

* * *

The next morning I went looking for Youssef who had said he would model for me at 10:30am, only to be told by some of his friends when I arrived at his shop that he was not expected until 11am. I was neither surprised nor terribly interested and without hesitation I returned to my hotel and swapped out my canvas for the portrait I had started at the gallery.

As I settled myself onto my usual stool it was as though no time had passed between the last time I had painted in their courtyard and the present. It was as if time was magically suspended there, an invisible bubble encased the gallery and kept the chaos of the outside world at bay. The same salesmen would always be sitting half asleep in antique chairs, sprawled across old hand carved sofas reading the paper and their contemporaries, the drowsing cats, would likewise be found perpetually curled up in odd corners. The same jokes and stories would be told to pass the time years after I had gone from them and yet, while I was there I was included and absorbed into their company with barely a ripple, not even a fluctuation in space. I became another languid denizen, except I counted the minutes in brush strokes.

I took my time until finally I sat back and the painting was done, the muted worn blue tones of the door faded into the background, a nearly vague side note given to establish placement, a certain atmosphere in its slanted indifferent angles. Looking at it, the viewer would not guess that its soft lines had taken me nearly three afternoons to put in, more time than the closer detailed focus of the painting, my glowing model.

After I packed up I retraced my footsteps and found an apologetic Youssef standing on his street corner. After negotiations I got him to agree to model for my price. He wanted 400 dirham for two hours and after I finished laughing at him I told him I paid all models in Essaouira the same, 150 dirham take it or leave it. I did wonder if there were silly enough European artists who would pay that outrageous price.

His family owned a couple of rug shops in one of the side alleys and he made me comfortable on a stack of rugs before sitting across from me in front of an old wood door. He wore a bright orange-red, worn t-shirt and had tied a blue scarf around his head. It was a strange mix of modern and traditional and I wondered if in its way it wasn't more authentic, more realistic then my requests for the Bedouin desert robes. I still could not help but feel annoyed by the t-shirt however. I didn't like the plain cut and I disliked the color. I felt it brought too many primary colors into the picture and not enough neutrals but I let it go, impatient to start so I could keep my appointment with Isham's aunt later.

I had barely begun when Youssef sighed and shifted and asked me to buy him a pack of cigarettes. I realized painting him would be a far different experience from painting Isham who I would have gladly bought cigarettes, but then he had earned my friendship. Youssef on the other hand had not yet proven himself. On my refusal, I was granted a few more minutes of silence then a sales spiel began meant to tempt me into buying rugs or perhaps painting his father next, a heavyset unshaven man who sprawled asleep across a couple of rugs. Or maybe I would be interested in painting one of his giggling cousins or uncles whose shadows doused my sketch in perpetual darkness as they leaned as close as possible in order to give Youssef a running commentary on my progress. When all sales pitches failed Youssef lapsed into silence but bored kept squirming and changing positions though when I asked he insisted he was comfortable.

Painting him was more of a struggle then all of the other models combined and halfway in I found myself feeling burnt out and impatient to be finished. I gritted my teeth and forced myself to focus, even as the pose changed once more. I had to concentrate and isolate what had not changed, what had remained consistent and map that in as I waited for him to return to the original pose unconsciously. There was no point in me lecturing him or trying to direct him back into the pose. I needed to be patient, to push my memory training, my knowledge of skull structure, facial anatomy, planes, angles, contours, balance that would bring one side of the face to match the other. I was lucky in that his face with its facial hair, well defined cheekbones, full mouth, shadowed jaw had many reference points which could be painted in quickly. It was the richness of his skin color that was the challenge, he was the darkest of all of my models and the mixtures I had become accustomed to mixing for their portraits would not work for Youssef. He had a black man's complexion and features but there were more golds, greens and reds in his skin then the deeper purples and blues of more African black men. He still had a hint of the Arab mixed in.

Slowly his face began to emerge out of the light brown base tone of my canvas. Behind his head I laid in the slightly darker walnut brown of the brass studded antique door that leaned unhinged against the stone wall behind him. As I breathed, I caught a whiff of spices on a sudden tickle of breeze and was aware suddenly of the way the daylight filtered down the pale walls, dancing across the surface of swaying tapestries which hung down the length of the alley. There was something magical about sitting on a pile of rugs in a Moroccan back alley. A quality to the experience that tasted haphazard and bohemian, a moment more out of a half waking dream then reality. Somewhere above my head a cat meowed forlornly and as I worked I pulled my legs in automatically to make room for passing carts and bicycles without my brush pausing.

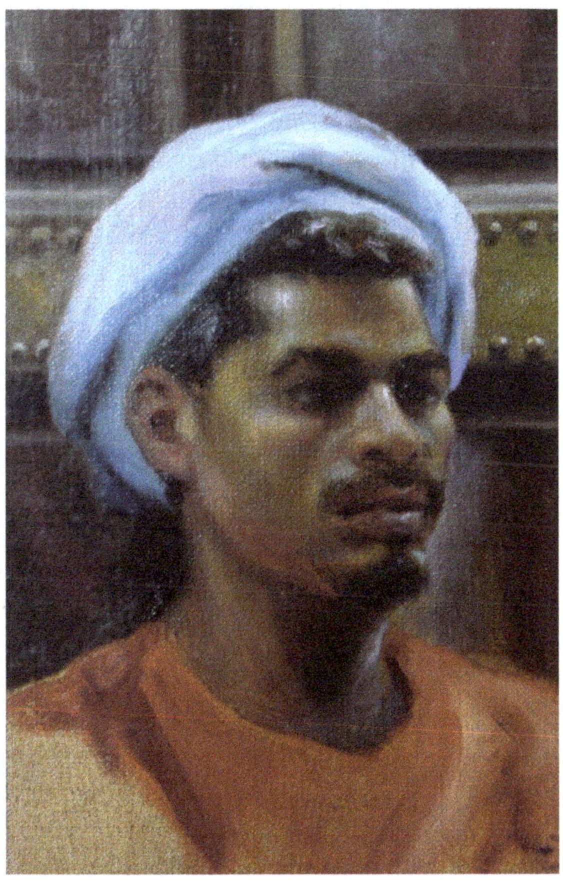

When the two hours were up I sat back and stretched, releasing Youssef with a wave. It was him on my canvas, definitely, staring off to the side, though too stiff for my liking. It didn't suggest any of his constant movement, his voraciousness of character. There was no sense of the alley behind him yet, nothing solid anyway and I knew I would have to return and endure him and his relatives again in order to put in a backdrop with any kind of dimension. I wasn't happy with the painting but it was too early I decided. I needed to look over the portrait later in my room and refine the anatomy, the passages of light, and the transitions into shadow.

I was headed back to my hotel, my hands full of wet paintings and all of a sudden heard the familiar, "Hey artist! Hey painter!" I cringed, imagining another would-be model and almost pretended not to hear but at the last minute stopped and turned around.

"Please, may we look?" It was a rug salesman who I had passed everyday with my varying canvases and after a moment of hesitation I handed them over.

"They are a little wet, the paint, so be careful."

He nodded and touched the boards only by the backs and edges as he held them out and away from him so the other shopkeepers who had gathered around him could also see. They talked softly among themselves, glancing up at me every now and then. "I know this man," he said jerking his chin at one of the paintings. "He works just there," he said with a nod toward the corner I had just rounded.

I smiled reluctantly, pleased. I was tired, my neck and shoulders ached, my eyes burned and my mind felt weary. Above all I wanted to be polite, I wanted to talk to the local people but part of me also wanted to hide away and retreat into silence, just to think and soothe my thoughts.

"How much do you charge, to make the picture?"

I blinked at him surprised, "I pay him to sit a few hours for me."

"Yes, but I would like a picture, I want you to paint my picture. How much?"

The other salesmen murmured and shuffled a little closer to hear my response. I swallowed hard, unsure of how to respond, I did not want to seem dismissive but my time in Essaouira was coming to an end very soon. I was also nearly out of canvas. We could do some sort of trade but not only did I not want another rug but I knew the sort of price he was thinking of was comparable to the prices the tourist art sold for in the mini galleries dotting the side streets. Somewhere in the neighborhood of 20 dollars or less, the difference alone in the quality and cost of canvas and paint I used was immense.

"I am sorry," I said slowly. "I am so busy and I leave very soon. If I have time I will come back and let you know but I don't think I will have time to do a painting of you."

He nodded and handed the paintings back, "but maybe if you have time...you come and tell me."

"Yes, I will. Thanks," I smiled and waved as I moved off. I could feel my shoulders beginning to hunch and my chin to tuck against the stares I could feel as I walked on. Suddenly I just wanted to get back to my hotel room, to shut the door behind me and collapse on my bed for just five minutes. Yet when I arrived I had just enough time to clean my brushes, remix my pools of paint and get a fresh canvas. I had decided the key to successfully painting outside of the studio was the prep work. Premixing paints beforehand saved an immense amount of time on location and allowed me to focus primarily on composition, light, and tone. Premixing was easiest if I had already had the opportunity to work with the model before and was familiar with their coloring but Isham's aunt Fatima, was a complete mystery. I still premixed some generic pools of paint that with any luck would work with minimal adjustments. It was also important to pay attention to packing materials so they were easily and quickly accessible in my day pack. I double-checked to ensure I wasn't leaving out something simple but hugely vital like paper towels or my palette knife.

Isham was waiting for me in front of his store and with a few words turned his shop over to his cousin and led me outside the medina walls to his family's house. When we arrived, his aunt had not yet returned from the market so her husband made me some mint tea while I sat on a heap of cushions in a small sitting room. With the first fragrant sip, I felt the nerve endings in my body spark briefly, brilliantly, then unspool, spiral out soft, softer, even as my mind began to clear. Shades, tones, combinations, mixtures, filbert brush strokes versus rounds, all the painting mechanics and variations finally blinking out one by one until I was warm and blank and the only thing I could sense was the sweet clearing taste of hot Moroccan mint tea.

When she walked through the door heavily laden with bags, her husband started to yell and berate her for being late but I emphasized with a lazy shrug of my shoulders that there was no problem. Isham said, "This is my aunt, Fatima, she does not speak English but I have explained to her that she will sit for you for a few hours. Then she will cook. When I return at sunset we will all eat together. I go now to my shop. Is there anything else you need?"

I looked around the windowless sitting room and said, "I need a room with natural light, the light from outside."

He turned to his aunt and spoke for a few minutes then turned back to me, "My aunt says her room has light. You will be here when I get back? We would be honored if you eat with us."

"Of course, I promise I will be here. I would be honored, I haven't eaten much traditional Moroccan food." I reflected back on my nightly meal of cheese pizza, because the pizza café was the only one open before the sun set and their prices were cheap. I breathed out a sigh, "I look forward to it."

The room Fatima shared with her husband had a single window set into the wall above her bed and I leaned over and opened it so a narrow shaft of sunlight spilled down the whitewashed wall. As she sat back against a pile of pillows I positioned for her, I took my place and readying my charcoal for a quick lay in, studied her. She was at first glance a plain, middle-aged woman clad in a serviceable white robe, her hair was covered by a simple multicolored kerchief and her face was uncovered. Yet the longer I looked at her, the more I saw: she had a smooth golden complexion, lighter than my other models and bright inquisitive eyes that followed my every move. She had an enchanting way of tilting her head back while cocking it to one side that suggested her consideration of me was as intent as mine of her. But there was also a kindness to her, a sympathetic feel in the angle of her brows, compassion in the relaxed line of her mouth. There was a beauty to her plainness. Her face seemed clear and open as though any emotion would cross it fully exposed, like a storm passing over the open flat plains, seen for miles before arriving and then blowing away in pure, clean gusts of wind and gentle, falling, silver rain. Her face was a little more difficult to capture than my other portraits, if only because the light was indirect and there were no clear shadows to divide the planes of her face. Her features were more subtle.

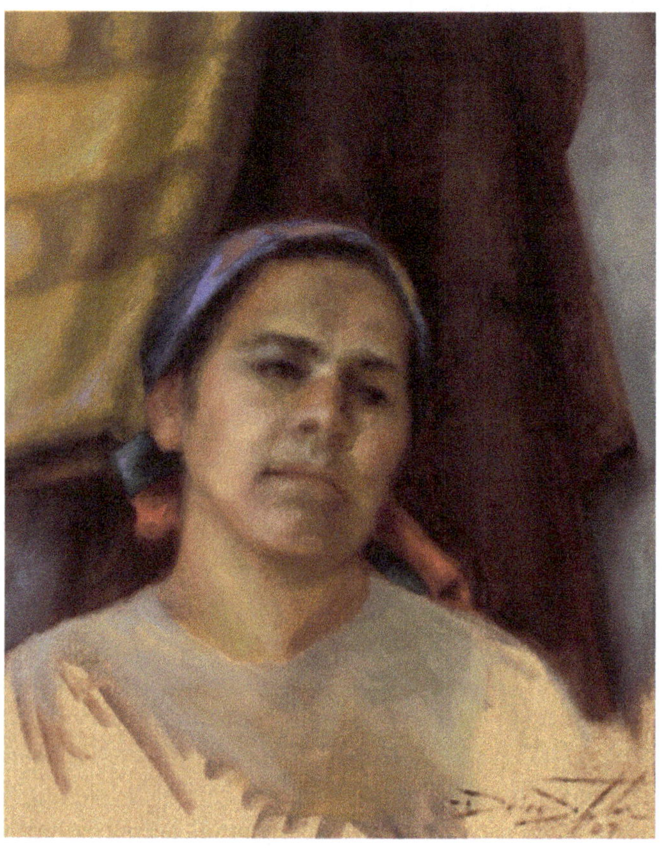

After a couple of hours I waved her up and after stretching, I rearranged the folds on the curtains which had framed her head and began to rework the background. I turned the painting to her so she could see herself and she shook her head and bent over to laugh, holding her stomach as she did, so the sound rippled through her as she gave herself over fully to it. She went and got her husband, who held the sketch at arm's length as he shook his head silently, the corners of his mouth twitching as though he were caught between amusement and amazement.

They left together after handing it back so I could finish in peace and considering it, it was her face but it seemed too solemn, her expression nearly tired, without that enchanting question mark which had sparked in her eyes. It was simple to put down features, technical details of light and shadow. To capture a feeling however, to express an observed emotion, something that was as intangible as a breeze and just as fleeting, was far more complex. It was as though I had to be a translator, to take something I could feel cross the space between us, an electric current that tickled the surface of the skin and to make the unseen, visual and translated through paint. Yet, it was one thing to feel and another to find the right combination of brush strokes to hold it and tame it to canvas.

I spent another hour refining the background until the light began to seep from the window, deepening in color before vanishing and Isham returned with a shout and clatter. We all sat down together as Ramadan broke at 6:30pm to eat. Fatima had made a thick savory Moroccan stew called tagine, made with beans, rice, and meat, followed by a plate of sticky Ramadan pastries with sesame seeds sprinkled liberally on top. These pastries were ones Adrian had recognized from Iraq that he and his soldiers had called camel turds because of their round spiraling shape, though they tasted of honey, syrup, and sunshine. She had not bought them at the market but had made them herself and Isham pointed out that hers were far better than any I would find for sale in the bazaar. When I finished I thanked them profusely and Isham walked me back to my hotel because he knew being out after dark by myself made me nervous.

* * *

"You want to know how to paint a perfect painting?
It's easy. Make yourself perfect and then
just paint naturally.
That's the way all the experts do it. The making of a painting or the fixing of a motorcycle isn't separate from the rest of your existence. If you're a sloppy thinker the six days of the week you aren't working on your machine. What trap avoidances, what gimmicks, can make you all of a sudden sharp on the seventh? It all goes together."
-Robert Pirsig, The Art of Motorcycle Maintenance

I wanted to start a new painting from the top of the wall of the Skala du Port the next morning but it did not open until 9:30am so I walked to a nearby bakery I had not yet tried and arrived right as they were putting trays of fresh pastries out in the front display window. I walked in and pointed out two pastries still hot from the oven, one with a dollop of cream on top and one that was shaped like an éclair with a garnish of sliced, glazed bananas. I ordered a pot of mint tea and sat in a little courtyard surrounded by walls covered with old black and white photographs, as well as original watercolors and oils of different scenes in Essaouira. Between the two types of paintings displayed, the watercolors the shop featured were the strongest. I had a great deal of admiration for watercolors. On the whole, they never managed to quite achieve the rich color and burning glow of oils but there was a soft, moody, translucent quality to them that when done correctly was magical. Most watercolor artists I had met seemed intimidated by the complexity of oils. Yet most oil painters struggled when trying to duplicate the quick precise dash of a watercolor brush without creating a layered muddy mess.

At the Skala du Port I found a square gap in the wall that was meant for a missing canon and was just big enough for me to sit cross legged in with my palette box on my lap. Directly before me the port was bustling with fishermen fixing nets and repairing boats, below me was a sheer drop to opaque green water, still enough that it held a reflection of the walls. The weather was perfect for painting, warm without being hot and the sky clear but without wind. The stone was warm beneath me and I could feel myself melting into the scene before me: the blue flaking paint of the small skiffs, the fraying ropes which tied the bobbing boats to the stained concrete blocks, the mounds of reeking net which carried the flavor of echoing, depths filled with a flick of shimmering fins and scales. I could have stayed all day but I had other projects to work on. Still I pushed farther than I normally would have and covered the canvas with a small piece of the afternoon, a memory of salt scented air.

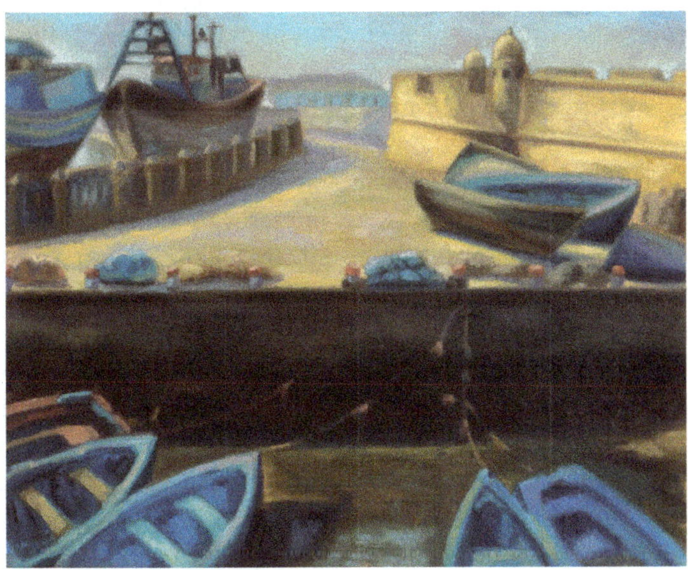

I went back to my hotel and completed the last two portraits that needed background resolution and touchups on the faces. I tried to work on the sketch of the sunset from my hotel window but finally decided it was a total disaster. My heart was no longer in it, the strokes were heavy handed and clumsy, the color was garish and indecisive. There was a light effect but it was too aggressive with none of the subtle twilit melting and merging of shadows that softens the last hour of daylight. I was exasperated by what was fast becoming a waste of materials but the subject was so beautiful I couldn't understand why the painting was so weak. My strength had always lain in the earliest part of the day, when not only my energy was greatest but my eye was freshest. The sunset painting had only received what was left over, the dregs of my weariness when everything began to blur and melt together and my power of observation was at its weakest.

I could sense the clock ticking. Deep inside of me I was already preparing to leave, disentangling my senses and stepping back. I had a hyperawareness of the passage of the sun and what it meant, that it was all getting closer to ending. It was a distraction which made it difficult to focus on anything else. Part of me missed the familiar and longed to be back in a country where I could drink water from the faucet and where the showers had the nozzle sensibly mounted to the wall, not loose so you had to hold it in your hand while lathering up clumsily with the other. My country, where I could trust the food not to get me so sick I would be left weak and shaking for days.

Yet, as the sun rises and the call to muezzin goes out over the city, as the fog lifts from the port, as the seagulls take to the air to inspect the catch brought in by the fishing boats, I will miss Morocco. Somewhere the sun is creeping up the length of the Saharan sand dunes, the snake charmers in el Fnaa are readying their flutes, and a small army of cats and kittens are scurrying into their appointed places watching for unattended food. Morocco is a country where even the poorest hotel has an ornately decorated lobby rich in tile work, a place where there is a potential model hanging out on every street corner, where every alley is a flash of color in undulating handmade rugs. I was almost ready to leave though. I could feel my thoughts pulling themselves from the scent of linseed oil and the feel of worn paint brushes and preparing for what lay ahead in the United States: a new job, a new state, a whole new living situation.

"But now, I miss the white, the black, the red, the brown faces of America. I miss their varied shapes, their tumultuous diversity, their idealistic search for racial equality, their bumbling but wonderful pioneering spirit. I miss English words in my ears, miss the way the language rolled off my tongue so naturally. I miss its poetry. Somewhere along the way, my search for roots has become my search for home- a place I know best."
–Andrew X. Pham, Catfish and Mandala

* * *

I sat on a concrete wall facing the ocean and the pale sandy beach. Behind me a wide concrete promenade served as a boardwalk and stretched in either direction in an illusion of infinity. It was warm but overhead thick rolling black clouds threatened more rain and there were no lounge chairs set up under the thatch umbrellas which dotted the beach. I had planned my last day in Essaouira very carefully and that plan had not included rain or being forced indoors. The beach was silent and vacant, the water a roiling grayish green the sheen and texture of fish scales, melding at the horizon with a mottled iridescent sky. To try to paint the transition from dark patches of cloud to the small fabric tears of blue would make for an interesting painting sketch, however I felt lazy. In the last ten days I had completed an unprecedented twelve paintings, for me an astounding number. I wanted nothing more than a leisurely day involving a good book, a kicked back cushioned chair in the shade facing the ocean, and a nap.

Even as I sat staring out at the water two French tourists walked up and had a Moroccan man go through a tower of covered chairs to find a book they had accidently left, probably the day before. After much unstacking and trouble the book was found with a wave of triumph by the Frenchman, and the Moroccan was duly tipped. He stood looking at his scattered chairs for a moment before beginning to restack them with an air of resignation. I approached hesitantly, hoping he understood English. When I spoke he started and stared at me with wide eyes before beginning to laugh and shake his head.

"I thought you were Moroccan sitting on the wall there with your book," he said with amusement and at my request pulled out a chair and cushion. I was short of cash and only had 22 dirham instead of 25 but he dismissed the difference with a smile and a shake of the head, undoubtedly I might be his only customer of the day.

I curled up with my journal and nearly an hour later he came by and saw me still scribbling madly away. "You must be writing a book about Morocco," he said laughing as he squatted by my chair. "Where are you from?"

I clutched my journal and huddled a little deeper in my jacket, "Alaska."

"Ah, very cold!" he said and patted my bare sandy foot. "If you need the bathroom, the one in the café, there," he pointed, "is free because you are my customer." He eyed me with affection and smiled, "You are a good girl, I could tell the first time I saw you. You enjoy, you are welcome here. If you need me, this is my name." He took my journal from me and carefully penned his name in the front cover, then with another approving nod he left.

As I looked out at the grey heavy sheen of ocean I thought about that phrase, 'a good girl.' I had tried very hard to cultivate that image and Isham had used the same words to describe me not long after we had met. That day as now I had on my standard attire, stained pants with rolled cuffs, a loose black shirt and heavy black jacket. My face was clean of makeup and my hair was tied neatly back. I also traveled with my mother's wedding ring on my left hand, a small simple band clean of stones or any ornamentation. An unmarried woman traveling alone was seen with less approval than a married woman traveling accompanied. Even with Isham I had pretended, though not entirely successfully, that my husband waited for me back at my hotel. Still, it was simpler to pretend to be married then to explain why I was not, or why I was traveling alone. A wedding ring was also helpful if I did not want to buy something, commit to a tour, or agree to dinner. I could always wave my left hand in the air and say I had to consult my husband. It worked fairly well until shopkeepers that I became familiar with day after day began to wonder aloud why I never brought my husband by, or why he never came to check on me as I painted. Other times, when the ruse could have proved most useful I forgot about it entirely.

The afternoon before I had found a café facing the port gate. There I could watch the late afternoon sun as it glowed off the rock walls and danced up from the paving stones of the square as I drank what could well be my last glass of Moroccan mint tea. It was mainly empty outdoor seating with a smattering of well-spaced tourists. Since Ramadan had begun the Moroccan men no longer sat at the cafes during the day which made it less intimidating to walk past them and easier to find somewhere to sit and drink tea without wondering if it was taboo. However, after only five minutes the seat next to mine had been pulled out with a scrape and a young Moroccan man grinning, had deposited himself into it. He had begun a series of insinuating salutations in French and I had stared at him in disbelief for a few minutes, eyebrows raised incredulously before leisurely turning my attention back to my book, speaking not a word. After a few more attempts he had finally left.

It was a technique I had found useful while traveling alone and being either solicited, cat called, or even flashed by men, which was if you gave absolutely no response at all they were more likely to leave you alone then if you spoke sharply to them. Their main goal was attention, even if it was negative. Speaking to them, even dismissively, let them know what nationality you were and I had found that all information about yourself while traveling should be given out with discrimination. Even after he had left however, I had felt like my peace was destroyed. I ruefully had twisted the wedding ring on my finger remembering that I should have held my hand up immediately for it to catch the light.

Remembering as I sat by the ocean, I wondered what had been expected of me, the choices another woman might have made. The skin on one of my fingers was stained with cadmium red, a brief flag of smudged paint, like a banner, a label, a true ring to mark what I belonged to.

Awakening From a Venetian Dream

7/17/01

I was lost among the tiny winding alleys of Venice when I passed a store and from the doorway came the strong scent of incense. I did not know the name or brand but it was the exact kind a friend of mine used to burn and I knew if I closed my eyes I would be sitting on his old wreck of a sofa in his apartment with the white Christmas lights he kept year around twinkling from his walls. All of that in a single breath of incense. All of that in a smell, but so familiar it was a taste, touch, and sound all in one and I wanted to be back in the United States so badly I could feel it blazing through me like fire. I walked faster, away from the scent because I was afraid if I paused I would run back and spend my last 9,000 lira on incense. That money was reserved for food only however, and had to last through the next day.

The reason I had only the U.S. dollar equivalent of four bucks left for food was because I had bought an opera ticket for my last night in Venice. I had purchased it from a girl in period dress standing on a street corner who said that the show was a collection of different arias by composers ranging from Mozart to Verdi, sung by performers in Renaissance costume. It seemed a fitting way to spend my last night in Italy.

Only one more day. I could sense it would be long because as it was it seemed like every minute dragged. It was strange to feel that way in a city as enchanting as Venice, but a year was a long time to spend away. Earlier I had spent hours painting a watercolor of one of the stone bridges soaring above the green water, the bright orange red bricks of the next door palazzo reflected perfectly in an upside down cascade of ripples. I had appreciated the decaying, faded decadence of Venice then. Half an hour later a gondolier drifted by and struggled to sing over the cacophony of a passing barge, a water taxi, and a fleet of bus boats. I had found myself annoyed again, wearied by the death of my illusions. In the past, envisioning Venice I had always imagined the canals choked with opera singing gondoliers as they poled their boats along, the rising notes of their voices the only sound to disturb the soft lap of water.

I returned to my hotel where outside my window six older Italian men played cards in the courtyard as thunder growled overhead. A wall of deep gray clouds rolled ever closer, though in the other direction the sky was a clear baby blue as far as the eye could see, dotted with soft white strips, like strands of cotton. I could remember in Florence playing cards all night with my friends. Drinking wine, smoking hash, one talented third year student would play until he was so drunk or stoned he would fall asleep at the table, cards in hand. If the rest of us had enough energy we would dig out our sketchbooks and charcoal and draw quick sketches of him unconscious, the better to tease him with the next day. He would eventually rouse himself much later with a sudden jerk of the head, eyes rising half-mast to announce that he was off to bed.

The games were highly competitive, scores rigorously kept and double checked, hands played in silence, interrupted only by low swearing or glares and smirks. Before cards it had been monopoly, an Italian board which became a problem any time someone landed on Community Chest or Chance. The card would be handed around, squinted at, and whoever read Italian best had to decipher it for the rest. Monopoly games lasted too long however, and tended to become volatile, resulting in bitter feuds. Now those friends were scattered. I hadn't bothered to keep the contact information of a single one of them. Like a gust of ashes on a tide of rising wind, burning memories, it was better to move on and not try to hold onto the past.

That night as I walked to the opera alone in my one good dress, listening to the purposeful sound my shoes made I thought of how I would never again have this moment. Some day if I returned to Venice even if it hadn't changed, I would be different and I would see it with different eyes. I would never again have this moment of anticipation alone in the dark night, a little lost with my small map and the ghosts of my expectations.

Chapter 7

Casablanca: Departures

"As far as one journeys, as much as a man sees, from the turrets of the Taj Mahal or the Siberian wilds, he may eventually come to an unfortunate conclusion-usually while he's lying in bed, staring at the thatched ceiling of some substandard accommodation in Indochina. It is impossible to rid himself of the relentless cloying fever commonly known as Home. After seventy-three years of anguish I have found a cure, however. You must go home again, grit your teeth and however arduous the exercise, determine without embellishment, your exact coordinates at Home, your longitudes and latitudes. Only then, will you stop looking back and see the spectacular view in front of you."

-Horace Lloyd Swithin Whereabouts

10/3/07

I lay listening with my eyes closed to the low chuckling murmur of a flock of pigeons and doves, a rumbling, ruffling purr of sound that created a ripple of air to tickle my eyelashes and let in a stream of silver light. I fought the temptation to get up. I was lost in that boneless sensation where my limbs did not yet belong to me because my body was still lost in sleep and my heart rate was still sunk deep into the well of my chest. It was that clear floating moment before thought fully penetrated.

I opened my eyes to my hotel room, walls painted a hopeful yellow, functional bed, not quite anonymous, yet not quite a home. I had left Essaouira by bus the day before and arrived in Casablanca late enough in the evening that I decided to settle in and continue my trip the next morning.

I decided to get up and explore the medina, the old original part of town. Yet when I finally emerged to prowl the streets I found no trace of Humphrey Bogart, or his smoky bar playing piano blues. The city of Casablanca was very modern and industrial but immediately deteriorated once inside the walls of the medina where the streets were covered in trash and the buildings became low and squalid. It made me nervous and I headed back toward my hotel in search of breakfast. At first the only businesses I could find that were open were travel agencies but finally I managed to find an open market and was able to buy yogurt and pastries.

An hour later my bus arrived on time and when it finally pulled into Rabat I hauled my bags up to the first taxi driver I saw and said with a sigh, "Rabat airport." He stared at me blankly and his other passenger told me there was no Rabat airport. I pressed the point until they both decided I must mean the Rabat/Sale airport, even though my plane itinerary only said Rabat. I rechecked my guidebook which was completely unhelpful and nervously got in. I was used to the Moroccan taxi drivers' habit of picking up and dropping off multiple customers and as he stopped continuously to pick up and let off new fares I counseled myself to patience. I had allowed myself plenty of time to get there. After awhile however, I recognized the walls of the medina of Rabat and realized we were nowhere near the airport and he had deliberately been stalling, driving me in circles, perhaps in the hopes of raising the price. When I confronted him finally he became evasive and asked that I pay him immediately. For the first time in my trip I felt myself losing my temper and I ended up getting out and catching a different taxi that refused to start driving until I paid him. I gave in with a snarl and got to the airport just in time for boarding despite the fact that I had given myself three hours for what should have been a forty-five minute drive.

In an almost symbolic gesture the stewardess walked through the cabin spraying the air with air freshener as I finished settling myself in. As the over-sweet chemicals hit my nose I could not help but feel as though she was trying to erase even the sensory memory of Morocco. Not only the chaos and frustration of the roads and taxis but the eastern spices, the grittiness of the streets and the earthy musk of the sun. It should have been comforting to be in the refined, civilized hands of Air France, but as the plane lifted off I pressed myself closer to the window for a last sultry glimpse.

Once in Paris I realized other than rigid unpadded metal chairs with arm rests to prevent the weary from stretching out, or the cold uncarpeted concrete floor, there was nowhere to spend my fourteen hour overnight layover. For an hour I walked from one end of the airport to the other looking for options because I couldn't afford the subway into town and a hotel priced in Euros. Finally I found an empty terminal with only one flight scheduled to arrive for the rest of the night. In front of long tables were moveable chairs that I could push in front of the metal fixed ones so I could put my legs up. A homeless man, a rather prosperous one from the quantity of bags in his wire shopping cart, cleverly stood on a chair and turned on a big screen TV high up that I did not even notice. If only I could have spoken French I would have asked, "Where is a good place to camp out around here at night?"

In my metal chair I sat and tried to think. I couldn't give up, I had to figure something out. I got up once more and going up an escalator found a cafe with a sitting area in front of it that was bordered by a large c shape of red vinyl benches with high cushioned backs. After a few offhand questions I discovered the café closed at 10pm. I bought a four dollar cup of tea served in a 12 oz. paper cup and nursed it for two hours, tipping the staff another dollar to get more hot water. When the café closed I and some other grim looking patrons swung our legs up and tried to go to sleep. I used my bag as a pillow and had already transferred all valuables from my pockets into my money belt which was tucked inside my pants, for safekeeping. Quickly enough all spots along the bench were taken.

It was only immediately noticeable who was a camped out tourist and who was homeless when the emergency evacuation siren went off around midnight. A robotic announcement broadcast that a bomb had been sensed and everyone was required to leave the building. Yet, only the tourists sat up and looked around nervously. However, the nearby maintenance crew didn't stop polishing the floor and the homeless didn't even twitch. I was afraid of relinquishing my hard won spot so I decided to wait and see if I would be bodily removed by security or consumed in a fiery explosion. After ten minutes however, the siren went quiet. The tourists returned to find their spots usurped by new homeless and I huddled a little deeper in my jacket, feeling grateful I had taken the chance. On one side of me a man with dirty bare feet snored softly and to the other side a man moaned and thrashed in his sleep.

I woke at 6:30 am just minutes before the staff gently touched each sleeping bundle on the shoulder. No sound was made as the homeless gathered their things and melted away even as the tourists got up to buy obscenely priced coffee. I had a crumbling Danish left from the market in Casablanca that I had saved for breakfast and with a shrug spent my last euros on a tiny coffee.

The plane engines growled to life and I settled back into the depths of my chair. It was already bleeding from me, the exact smell of Morocco, the color, the people. I had carefully put my loose finished canvas paintings into my carry-on and I could feel them like a human presence, crouched by my feet and sending soft waves of comfort and purpose. Soon I would be back, another faceless waitress, hands full of dirty plates, mind blank, smile fixed firmly, stiffly in place but my heart would still be thousands of miles away lost in the scent of paint and the cry of ocean gulls.

There was a choice to be made I realized. I could return and lower my head, settle myself into the invisible traces, and pretend as though Morocco had never happened so that I would not mourn too greatly my new surroundings. Or I could bring Morocco with me. I could layer myself in Mexico and Italy. I could dust my eyes with the gleam of my collected countries. My gaze could hold a misty horizon of the Sahara, my smile a taste of tagine and fresh dates, my hair the scent of spices from the bazaar and my feet could move to the beat of an invisible snake charmer's drum. As winter set in I could cloak my body in the comforting heat of Mexico. Every time I thrust my time card into the squalling mechanical time clock I could hear instead the call of Arturo's band of mariachis rising in the night above the town of Batopilas. I could remember how the stars above my head were the same stars that shone above the ancient city of Teotihuacan, and that the looming sun and moon pyramids did not count time only endured it.

I had a choice to make. If I could hold it all within me, the scent of painting medium, the rough texture of canvas, the gritty touch of charcoal, none of it would ever be lost. I could hold eternity within. Morocco would be all around me. Every night the sun would set in Italy and the rest of the world would be waiting just around the corner.

Open the Door

"We write to taste life twice, in the moment in retrospection... we write to be able to transcend our life, to reach beyond it. We write to teach ourselves to speak with others, to record the journey into the labyrinth"
-Anais Nin

To my fellow artists out there, those of you who feel you have something to express, something to say with your paints and notebooks and musical instruments and all other tools of inspiration. The classroom teaches so much; tearing yourself away and standing outside the front door can be overwhelming. Instead of the sympathetic eye of your instructor and fellow students, you are putting your art and yourself out there for the whole world to see and judge, and they will. How many times have I been in some alley somewhere trying to capture a fleeting light effect with my paints and every five minutes some passerby had to stop, try to engage me in conversation and give me their opinion? Well, all I can say is, it's part of the experience. Wear headphones and ignore them, or pause to talk and find yourself making a new friend.

There will always be endless complications. A big one is getting your materials on and off planes without them being confiscated, lost or stolen. And if the worst happens? Should you call off your trip?

What if you get out there, having spent a small fortune on transportation and supplies and all that you create suddenly seems terrible? Time in school feels wasted because suddenly you have no idea how to approach your subject. Where do you start? What in the heck are you doing? Doubt is a wonderful thing. I became an artist not to make money, not to be the next Da Vinci, but because drawing and painting were like breathing. I couldn't imagine trying to live without it.

Hold onto your passion and step outside of your safe, comfortable, air-conditioned studio. Go somewhere where you can't speak the language. Lug around a ridiculous number of supplies and I promise you a confusing, scary, intoxicating experience. Don't worry about the quality of the work you create, remember why you became an artist in the first place and hold onto that. Creating in the studio environment means you are relying solely on the contents of your mind to furnish your work, but the world holds much that can only find its way into your soul if you see it with your own eyes.

Acknowledgements

Thanks for tirelessly editing the first drafts of my manuscripts, JoAnn Baker Contreras and Philip Dempster. I couldn't have done this without you.

About the Author

Deirdre has traveled to over 30 different countries, often alone, and is thoroughly captivated by travel. When Deirdre isn't traveling, she tends bar in a small town in Arizona where she lives with her husband. In spite of going to school at Westminster College, the Corry Studio of Figurative Art, the Art Institute of Southern California, Saddleback College, The Florence Academy of Art, Whatcom College and Rio Salado College, she received her Bachelor of Science degree in Humanities from Northern Arizona University. Even as she pursues her Master's degree in Professional Writing, she makes time to paint almost every day and to dream of her next trip.

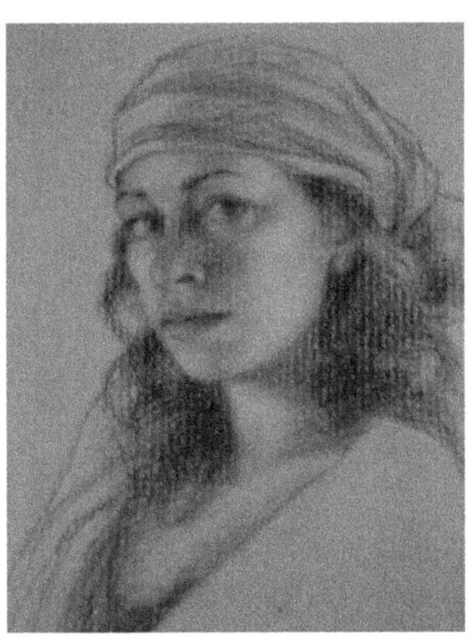

www.ingramcontent.com/pod-product-compliance
Ingram Content Group UK Ltd.
Pitfield, Milton Keynes, MK11 3LW, UK
UKHW021827270726
14058UKWH00001B/9